SOMETHING IS HAPPENING

A much-respected figure in the human potential movement explores the way the unconscious impinges on our everyday behaviour and its relationship to the religious impulse.

SOMETHING IS HAPPENING

Spiritual Awareness and Depth Psychology in the New Age

by

WINIFRED RUSHFORTH O.B.E.., M.B., Ch.B.

TURNSTONE PRESS LIMITED
Wellingborough, Northamptonshire

First published March 1981
Second Impression November 1981

British Library Cataloguing in Publication Data

Rushforth, Winifred
Something is happening
1. Psychology, Religious
2. Religion and Sociology
I. Title
306'.6 BL53

ISBN 0-85500-149-6

Typeset by Ad' House, Earls Barton, Northamptonshire.
Printed in Great Britain by Nene Litho, Earls Barton,
and bound by Weatherby Woolnough,
Wellingborough, Northamptonshire.

Contents

Page

Introduction 9

Chapter

1. Psychology and Religion – A Personal Note 11
2. A Map of the Psyche 17
3. The Light and the Dark: Yin and Yang 29
4. The Unconscious 35
5. Repression and Analysis 43
6. The Wound and its Healing 49
7. 'My Illness': The Interdependence of Body and Spirit 57
8. What About Dreams? 67
9. Guilt and Forgiveness 81
10. Do You Love Me? 89
11. The Seven Deadly Sins 95
12. Aspects of Aggression 107
13. Being Content to Not-know 117
14. Old Age 127
15. The Emergence of Human Potential 135

Epilogue: The Lord's Prayer 147

Acknowledgements

My gratitude to those who have helped me to write this book stretches back fifty years or more to the time when the work of understanding human nature became of increasing importance to me.

My great debt is to the patients who have entrusted me with the exploration of their problems in relationship, involving love, hate, resentment, remorse, guilt and forgiveness. It is they who have made this book possible.

I am indebted also to Alick Bartholomew for his belief in the value and worthwhileness of what I have tried to say. Jessie Reid has put a great deal of work into helping to prepare the manuscript and correct the proofs; but I would thank her even more for pointing out to me, early in our friendship, that I was not writing a text-book in psychology but a personal testimony. Special thanks go to my artist friend Jessie May Stirling for making the Map of the Psyche visible and therefore more vivid than my writing could do.

I would also mention in particular Andy Sluckin, who did valuable editorial work in the later stages, and Jane Carre, who so willingly typed many of the early drafts. Both have been more than generous. May they and all the others who have helped me know that I am most grateful.

M.W.R.

Introduction

I have put off writing this book although the urge has been there for many years. I have longed to share what has seemed to be 'good news' – some sort of gospel – with others, but have held back till now – my 96th year. I have questioned whether I have one thing worthwhile to say, anything that other folk have not said many times. I have, perhaps arrogantly, wanted to present original truth, but now realize that truth lies deep in the unconscious of each of us, 'at the bottom of the well', and that it is there all the time for us if we are willing to go to the well to draw water.

This book sets out to deal with the unconscious life, the 'hinterland' of our existence, and with my own attempt to explore it. Others, of course, from the beginning of time have wandered away from the known into the unknown, aware of the horizons but questioning what lies beyond, where a great wealth of wisdom has been discovered and is available today. Available? To the philosophers perhaps, to the students of the sciences, to specialists in many fields of knowledge. We, however, the ordinary folk, parents, teachers, office workers, craftsmen, artists – categories of ordinary people, the individual whom we call 'the man in the street' – what access have we to all this knowledge, wisdom, understanding, produced through the centuries, more available today through the media than ever before in mankind's history, but still often hidden and undiscovered?

Modern psychology is strangely co-existent with my own lifetime. Freud was already working with Pierre Janet in Paris when I was born in 1885. Jung was only ten years older than I. Freud and Jung went together to New York in 1909. Adler, a contemporary of Freud from Vienna, went to the States in the 1930s and drew huge audiences to listen to his popular teaching on the understanding of human nature, which must have been the source of much acceptable psychology on that side of the Atlantic. Hitler's great dispersal of the Jews in the later part of that decade took many eager adventurers in this field into new territory. We remember with gratitude the names Bruno Bettleheim, Viktor Frankl, Erik Erikson, Karen Stephen, Karl Sheru, and realize how their teaching has come back to Britain, enormously enriching our comprehension of the nature of life, giving us some clues towards the solution of its problems.

I offer my contribution with humility, aware that it is in no sense a text book, not authoritarian in any way. It is the by-product of my contact at deep levels, with people of both sexes, of different nationalities, all ages, people as parents, people as children – husbands, wives, masters and servants, physicians and their patients. All of them have become in some measure aware of difficulty in their lives – unfulfilment, frustration, suffering of body and mind. For fifty years and more I have been listening and learning, always with faith in the healing process, aware of the great virtue of life energy when it is free in our lives, when we can take it and hold it and give it again: take from the source; hold in our own health and sanity; give again and again to those who come for healing, for new vision, new life-patterns. Each patient has rewarded my ability to listen by adding some grain of wisdom to my psyche. In fifty years much has accumulated that urges me to find others in need whom I can reach through my writing. I send the book out into the world hoping that from it, too, there may be a *diaspora* – a scattering of seed that will find good ground in the heart of you the reader, and bring forth a good harvest.

Edinburgh, September 1980

1.

Psychology and Religion — A Personal Note

We often forget how recently the word psychology has come to be used in common talk. The Oxford Etymological dictionary, defining it as the science of the human mind, states that its use is only occasional before the nineteenth century. I have a personal recollection of hearing the word for the first time in 1922 when a friend from London, who was visiting me in Calcutta, spoke of lectures in psychology which had been a part of her teacher training. They had certainly not been included in my medical curriculum which dated back to the first years of this century (1903-1908).

In 1927, however, I was asked to give psychological lectures to Health Visitors in Calcutta. When I protested that I had neither training nor opportunity for preparation in this area, the Director of Public Health for Bengal assured me that his library was open to me and that as no other lecturer was available, he was eager for me to undertake the work. Hopefully, I collected a dozen volumes from his shelves, but hopelessly I discarded them on reading such misleading platitudes as 'obedience is the bedrock of child training' and such advice to parents as the best method of punishment for bedwetting and masturbation. I knew that these views were misguided and useless to me, but where was I to look for help? There were no popular books on child development, and the plethora of psychological advice which now comes to us daily through the media was then non-existent.

I shall always be grateful to Professor William MacDougall, a Scotsman from Lorne who emigrated to the USA and taught at Duke University, North Carolina. His book *Character and Conduct of Life* came into my hands – by chance it seemed at the time– and in it I found the material I needed for my lectures to the Health Visitors. Three years later, in 1930, I attended his 70th birthday party in London and was able to tell him how I had used his teaching in India. MacDougall was a contemporary of Freud. I do not think that Freud and Jung or Adler were mentioned in his book, but in common with them he taught that man's *instinctual equipment* was identical with that of the animals and that we must recognize and not be ashamed of our creaturely endowment. On this basis, and with some help from Adler's books, which were then available, I was able to prepare and deliver these elementary lessons in Calcutta. I then found myself eager to share what I was learning with other women – both European and Indian – who were mothers of young children and often found themselves in great difficulty. I had two such groups running concurrently in Calcutta in 1928/29. Later in 1929 I was accepted for training in analytic therapy at the Tavistock Clinic in London and I have been working almost without intermission in this field till the present day.

Although the word psychology did not come into my vocabulary until the 1920s, I can now realize how psychologically important the teaching of the Bible has been to me all my life, and especially latterly in my old age. Now that I am old I have a strange desire, almost a compulsion, to read and re-read the scriptures, annotating them, gathering the wisdom from the earlier writings, through the Old Testament into the New; correlating the teaching of Moses, who taught of the presence of Jehovah with his people, with that of St John and St Paul, who knew so clearly that the Christ is in us, our strength, our security and our 'hope of glory'. The Bible undoubtedly teaches us good psychology. It warns us against identification with the *persona* or mask – the front we present to the world – and teaches us to find our centre, the real self, by relating to the Creative Spirit which we call God. The notion of dependence on this 'not ourselves' links the teaching of the Bible to the teaching on which analytic psychotherapy is based, namely the possibility of access to unconscious forces, latent in each individual, awaiting full development in conscious life.

When in 1939 I met Jung in Oxford, just before the outbreak of World War II, I remember the insistence of his words as he addressed the assembled psychiatrists. '*This* is your insanity,' he told us, 'that you have lost your religion.' Religion and psychology were to him, and are to us, two aspects of man's search for truth. Long before we could spell 'psychology' we were comforted by Moses' message to the Israelites: 'Underneath are the everlasting arms.' Moses urges his people to go into all the depths, through all the fears and panics. *Ultimately*, he assures them, the foundation of all life is the holding love through which we conquer anxiety and fear and find the basic security which is so blessed an end to our seeking.

St Paul also deals with anxiety, in his letter to his fellow worker Timothy. He calls anxiety 'the spirit of fear'. Fear, itself instinctual, common to man and beast, serves a useful purpose as a warning to deter us from danger and destruction in the 'here and now' situation. Anxiety, the 'spirit of fear', serves no such useful purpose. It derives from experiences of fear and insecurity in early life, attaching itself irrationally to present events and to future ones, which of course need not take place. Psychologists talk of 'free-floating anxiety', indicating a state of mind ready to attach fear indiscriminately and irrationally to any circumstance. Paul's words are 'God hath not given us the spirit of fear, but of power and of love and of the sound mind.' Let us realize what he is saying! *Either-or*– 'Either live with anxiety or discover another way of life in which you will find energy, good relationships and tranquillity.'

To how great an extent could the so-called National Health Service become obsolete were we able to lay hold on that way of living! We use only a fraction of the energy available to us. We have not learned to love our enemies, and we swallow tranquillizing pills by the million, and all because we do not accept the basic security available.

I believe that our lives *can* be different. We must seek, as Freud has taught us, to recover lost memories of the events that so frightened us as children, but, also *in the here and now*, we must lay hold on the assurance of indwelling creative life – the *Not-I* – ever directing our steps towards the kingdom where love, not fear, reigns. Then, 'not guilty', we can live without the anticipation of punishment, without looking over our shoulders, dreading discovery and retribution, without asking: 'Is something awful going to happen?' When we accept forgiveness, then indeed something has happened, and we can 'take up our bed and walk' and return to the stream of creative life, activity and usefulness.

I have a fantasy – share it with me – of a healing Christ walking through the wards of a psychiatric hospital, smiling almost mockingly at the patients as he makes his rounds. Today he has taken the place of the Chief and his attendant white-coated young physicians, with the nurses and others who make the daily round. The Christ holds out his hand to one forlorn patient who day by day has hoped that the Chief would notice him and bless him. Almost laughingly the Christ says: 'Sonny, Lassie, what are you doing here? Don't you *know* that you needn't bother about that misdeed, that folly, that wrong thing you did? Now you are understood and need not feel bad about it any longer, you are not going to be punished.' 'Am I really not guilty?' says the patient as he jumps to his feet and turns his back on the hospital scene. Others hearing the same words of understanding and forgiveness know they need wait no longer, and soon the hospital wards are emptying themselves, and the erstwhile patients are following the Healer out into the world, to discover how best they too can learn to understand and heal.

Poor Chief and his white-coated staff! Unemployed, will they now take the plunge and commit themselves to 'the way of understanding' which we call therapeutic analysis? If so, they too will become healers, and the psychiatric hospital, so dreaded by the neurotic, psychotic, depressed members of our society, will be lit up with the Divine Healing Light. We shall flock to its doors begging for admission, not only to find healing but also to discover our true potential, the hidden gifts which can be of such great benefit to our neighbours and it may be to the world.

In the early days of my own life-time and indeed until I was a middle-aged woman, the so-called Mental Hospitals were also designated 'Loony Bins' and their doors might well have had the superscription 'All hope abandon ye who enter here.' It is different today – very different. The hospitals are equipped with a great armamentarium of drugs which alleviate the suffering, alter the painful emotional state, enable the patient to return to the community, but their approach to the healing power emanating from psychic unconscious processes is, all too often, completely lacking.

Once in my lifetime (once only so far) I had the experience of seeing a patient who had been sent to me as a hopeless case of multiple sclerosis, and had spent much time in hospitals, suddenly rise from the psychoanalytic couch and ask me 'Where is the light coming from? The whole room is full of light. Do you not see it?' It was a dark day in February – no light was coming in at the window. 'It's warm, it's lovely, can't you feel it?' As she put on her coat and left the room she said, 'I am going to see my mother.' The mother had rejected her child, who had known herself unloved and insecure and was consequently the victim of illness. The patient forgave her mother and this was the seal of her recovery. Six years have passed without recurrence of her illness. Mary tells me that she is never ill nowadays, that she is in touch with work for invalid children where she is useful. More interesting still do I find her statement 'I am never cold.' Something certainly has happened to Mary, healing psyche and body, both transformed when the light shone on her that dark day and she was able to go out and forgive her mother. Something happened the day that light filled the analytic room and now, through Mary, something is happening in her environment and great courage is given to you and to me to seek daily the way of understanding.

2.

A Map of the Psyche

From infancy to old age insistent problems of the whence and whither of our lives force themselves upon us– we ask questions of our parents, our nurses, our teachers, school-fellows. Will the Church with its priests and ministers have the answer for the adolescent? Will the university faculties of theology or psychology provide answers?

Some of us in old age are still wondering, questioning, not yet wholly satisfied with the answers or maybe repudiating them, giving up hope that the answers will come, content to not-know, dimly aware of great strata in which we have given up all attempt to enter. Let us verbalize again some of the questions of childhood and adolescence.

Where was I before I was born?
How did I get here?
Why did I come to be *your* child and not our neighbours?
Where is Heaven?
Why can't we see God?
What makes me tick?
Where is yesterday?

Where do I go when I am asleep?
Have I a beginning and an ending?
Is there a goal, is life purposeful?

These and many other things we want to know are still pressing upon us. As infants (the derivation of the word implies lack of speech) we have a great need to know, great urges towards discovery, a great need to find our *milieu* in the world which stretches its boundaries as our lives develop. It will help us in our thinking if we represent the psyche – our mental and spiritual being – by a map such as the one on the opposite page. Together now – as I write and as you read – can we see ourselves (as quite important people!) existing between two great areas, only dimly aware that our lives are in touch with these two infinite circles – the world of inner reality – let us figure it on our left since it has to do with the heart – and the world of outer reality – on the right as we stretch out the right hand towards the world of our neighbour. 'I am' – in Latin 'ego sum': *I exist* – places me here, midway between the two worlds. I am alive in this position. Let us stop for a moment and be aware of the throb of the heart and the body rising and falling as we breathe. I am – I am – what makes me tick? Whence the life energy? No longer 'infant', can I postulate a source, the Ground of all Being, cosmic, infinite, never to be measured or defined – invisible, intangible, unknowable – that is *unconscious*? Yet in it we live and move and have our being. (Three little fishes swimming in the sea met a great wise fish. 'Where are you going?' he asked. 'We are searching for the sea. In your wisdom, old fish, tell us where to find it.')

Francis Thompson has written:

Does the fish soar to find the ocean
The eagle plunge to find the air
That we ask of the stars in motion
If they have knowledge of thee there?

So now let us postulate that in this great inner world, unconscious, lies the Source, *fons et origo*, of all being. We may liken it now to the energy originating in a great hydro-dynamic location in the mountains where the dammed-up potential of

MAP OF THE PSYCHE

The ground of our being, the world of inner reality, the Unconscious.

The Dream
Archetypes
Animus, Anima
Racial Experience
The Instincts
Libido, Id Forces
The source of
Creative Energy
The Self
I need. I want
Life Force
God

The Cellar
EGO
I am
conscious
here
and now
Defence
Persona
Mask

Idealised Self-Image
Thou shalt, Jahweh
Thou shalt not The Law
Parents
You ought Neighbours
You must Teachers
Community
You ought not Police
You must not Nation
Civilization

The world of outer reality
Super-Ego forces

water awaits transmission as electricity into our cities, into our homes and workshops, endowing us for our daily living with heat and light and power.

Between the source and the light-bulb many transformers are needed. Cosmic power in its primitive onrush would be completely destructive – no heat or light or power but only darkness and chaos. What are the transformers? Always let us remind ourselves of our 'not-knowing', our 'agnosis', that the unconscious literally has depths of wisdom into which humanity cannot penetrate, but that we can become aware of some of them. Evolution working through the aeons with its significant variations has transformed life dramatically, taking no heed of time (God has made plenty of it). The great wars of history, shattering much that must have seemed stable, the anticipation of nuclear disaster today threatening civilization – so little we can understand. Again in human individuals transformation occurs – it may be with loss in all fields – loss of property, of friendship, of vision or hearing. There may be illness, the body may be rendered immobile through injury. Many happenings transform our available energy and we must constantly want to know what happens to us as we lay hold on life energizing the day to day activity.

To sleep is to become unconscious and as we yield to this process we create the dream which, as we awake, brings us wisdom and urges us to attend and be aware of this life-giving flow, in touch with the past, present and future time, in touch with primitive energy. It is in touch with that force which we call love interweaving through men and women everywhere, annihilating distance and nationality, affording us strange coincidence or synchronicities which jolt us into a marvellous awareness that *'we are one another'.* In psychological language this oneness is referred to as the collective unconscious and although it may seem a mystery it becomes more and more certainly part of Inner Reality.

The archetypes also inhabit this realm of the unconscious and personify themselves through the dream. Perhaps we best understand them by recognizing them as persons in our dreams. Firstly, of supreme importance, the contra-sexual figures. These are for the man the *anima*, his femininity, his intuitive wisdom, that through which he comes to his full capacity and creativity – provided always that he knows her as his comforter (in the literal sense of strength-giver), his guide, leading him, showing him the way. When his relationship of freedom and equality does not develop we find *anima* as cruel, hindering man's growth into maturity, imprisoning him in his childish patterns of impotence and guilt.

For a woman there is *animus* – contra-sexual, the masculine element in herself, again 'comforting', leading, guiding, giving her energy, increasing her capacity for understanding, her vitality, her strength. But negatively? Freudians rudely call her the 'penis woman' – 'as good as any man'. Not content with her intuitive wisdom, her capacity to love and understand, she tries to take over command – in family, household, business, government, she brings disaster rather than salvation.

Meeting the archetypes in our dreams can we recognize them as unknown parts of ourselves? We dream of pregnant women and new born babes – can we take it that something is happening within, that we are being born again, new life ahead of us? We dream of death – but in the unconscious there is no death only the body is disposed of. In the unconscious all things live, the psyche is immortal. It does not die but takes to itself another body, and another as it works towards maturity and fulfilment, existing, as it does out of time in aeonic eternity.

People of all ages come into our dreams and we learn to recognize ourselves as babes or aged, as young and sturdy, as old and wise. We may be invalids or physicians – 'Each man in his time plays many parts.' In appreciating and interpreting our dreams we learn to figure out what message these archetypes bring to us, recognizing that these figures carry the enlightenment, speak with honesty, always releasing energy from the Source, making it available in our lives and, using us as their vehicle, deploy their gifts in the world of humanity where there is so great a need.

In the apocryphal book of Ecclesiasticus the seer writes, 'I, like a conduit from a river, like a water course running into a garden, I said I am going to water my orchard, I intend to irrigate my flower-beds, and see my conduit has grown into a river and my river has grown into a sea.' His words convey to us some of the mystery of what is happening in our lives when we seek 'That' from which all life springs. Direction and purpose are implied in the inner life. Arising from the Source is the great flow directed outwards through the individual as channel into the outer world of Humanity and all life's happenings. Psychological language gives this flow the name *libido*. Freud, seeing the greatest importance in life to be the continuance of the species of man through the body, taught that it was predominantly sexual, creative through its genitality. In contact with Groddeck, a wise German physician, he termed it the *id* (the *it*) working in the body, in the case of illness and 'accident' destructively, but also with a healing restorative function.

Call it what we may, libido, id, psychic energy, we see it seeking its way into life, with creative evolving purpose – if it could speak, its word would be *I need* or *I want*. Lacking words, the infant makes his need known in his screaming or wailing. Once he can talk we hear 'I want' constantly on his lips. It is the language of the libido, but we deny him the use of it (stupidly, maybe, saying, 'I want gets smacked bottom'). In such ways we put obstacles in the flow of his libido, his creative energy, without which he finds himself listless, apathetic, enfeebled, lacking his birthright of aggressive vitality.

Leaving in the meantime this world of inner reality, let us construct in our map the other side, outer reality, visualising the *ego* placed between the two worlds, conscious of its own existence, saying 'I am, I am'. We may see it as a keystone balanced and held in position by the opposing forces of outer and inner worlds – let us call them superego- and id-energies, and we find the words Freud taught us to use 'superego;ego;id' the three forces existing in the psyche. Forces? Energy? All life ultimately, so the scientists tell us, is energy. Matter itself is energy. So 'ego sum' 'I am' is also a unit of this same power, surging into our lives.

After a child is born and the cord connecting him to his mother is cut, a process of disengagement is established and develops, and he becomes aware – at first very dimly aware – of the world into which he has been born, his outer environment, outer reality.

Fortunate children are kept in close relationship with the mother through the breast-mouth contact after birth so that the suffering of being 'an outsider' is considerably mitigated. In the womb he has been omnipotent, everything he needs has been provided without any vocal demand. She has given and he has taken in a completely harmonious situation. Birth involves separation, with a breakdown of this 'continuum' and consequent anxiety on the part of the child. His task now is to adjust himself to this new environment much as we do when we enter a foreign country and have to learn its customs, its laws and its language.

Intuition, the primitive knowing, must be already there at conception in the zygote, the cell incorporating both parents which develops into the embryo, the foetus, the human child.

Feeling develops in contact with maternal feeling, mediated to the developing life through the endocrines in the bloodstream, subject to her emotions, be they loving, accepting, rejoicing in her pregnancy or on the other hand sadly fearing, hating, rejecting the life in her womb. Man's *sensory* function also awakens in the womb. As the embryo quickens and moves in the amniotic fluid, awareness develops, his skin registers touch, his limbs register movement, through his ears he becomes aware of the drum-beat of his mother's heart and even of the ticking sounds of his own.

In the moments, hours, days, weeks, after birth immense experience impinges on the babe and in his response to it he changes, his psyche develops, his body asserts itself with incredible speed and he takes on his individuality, becoming a person, in whom we can observe the birth of *thought*. No longer are his responses merely conditioned, but the human faculties of choice and decision-making become evident. We can see his hands reaching out, grasping, selecting objects, repeating maternal movements. He is recognizable as an individual unit of the human race, unique in his inheritance, unpredictable in his potential. For all we know he carries in him 'a significant variation' through which the course of mankind's development may change for good or for evil. He is a growing point in the race asking us to handle him gently, with reverance, wonder and love.

At this point, his entry into the outer world at birth, he meets demands made upon him which, using Freud's language, we call the super-ego and now we see on our map three areas – super-ego; ego; id. Each of them has a word attached – I ought; I am; I want. We now look further at this *outer* superego area of the psyche.

The first 'ought' to the new-born is spoken by the mother,

reinforced by the mothers of the past, saying that the child *ought* to sleep, to wake, to feed, to excrete, to conform to patterns established. Neighbours join the family and as he grows the community add their voices enjoining conformity – approved behaviour brings the child the label, good, but if disapproved he earns such epithets as difficult, problem, naughty, yes *bad*. (Poor child! Has no-one noticed that it is the parents, the family, the setting of his life that are difficult and create his problems?)

School reinforces super-ego demands. The child must learn what is 'the done thing' and must obey the rules. His efforts to break away bring disfavour and punishment. Social workers and police reinforce the community standards– ultimately civilization enforces the 'you ought' of right behaviour.

Just as the inner world has deep within it an ultimate 'ground', so here too we look beyond society to find Jehovah, the God who from the heights of Mount Zion gave the rabble slaves in the wilderness the Ten Commandments – each with its 'ought', its 'Thou shalt; thou shalt not' – enjoining obedience and morality through which they were disciplined and became a nation. Today 'morality' still plays a part in our lives even when we do our best to close our ears to its voice.

Are there two 'Gods' in our map? One in the depth and one on the heights? Our map must take on spherical dimensions and, like Copernicus, we shall discover that the Sun illumines the earth through all seasons, by day and by night– and that 'I want' becomes 'I am willing' and that through the commandments we begin to glimpse the will of God in which mankind finds peace.

Super-ego demands, then, beginning with family discipline may meet with enlightened education, and a civilization not too drastic in its regulation of individual behaviour. From the beginning of life it matters whether love and intuitive wisdom discipline the children or whether 'text-book rules' and fear of 'what the neighbours think' are the guiding principles. Discipline– we envisage the super-ego in this role– is essential: without it an unruly 'id' would bring havoc into the situation and the balanced structure be demolished. Physically, parents, neighbours, school masters, do not go with us through our life; but what they represent in the disciplinary influences are taken into the psyche, internalized and, all too probably, we are at their mercy throughout life. The parental 'you ought' and even 'we ought' insinuates itself into the impressionable child and he now reacts with 'I ought'. The super-ego has taken up its abode within. Gentle efficient control, administered by loving understanding parents, gives freedom and allows for initiative and we see the happy child who is developing into a creative adult of great value in his community. On the other hand harsh rules, endorsing so-called good behaviour, beget adults who suffer from the rigid imposition of law. They lack the spontaneity and sense of being guided by wisdom and energy deriving from the Source with its flow that seeks to bring us as human beings into awareness, consciousness of 'That' the creativity so infinitely more valid than ourselves. Let us keep in mind always the human function as channel, pipe-line, live wire – deriving its energy from the Source.

From the Source, then, is always emanating a life-giving energy seeking its way through the individual into society, into human life, into the world. Wise parents relate to this by intuition, or it may be through meditation and the practice of God's presence. Wherever, whenever this wise and gentle parenthood is becoming a reality more children are born and reared whose lives will be creative. For the others – do not let us despair – the message of life is that of rebirth. Many secrets still lie hidden in the deep unconscious. In words given us even before Christ's coming we are taught that God's love and His pity redeem. Through them we are brought back, new born, into the creative life-stream, accepted as the sons of God, chosen to fulfil His purpose.

Now we must add to our map further structures which the super-ego activity imposes on the psyche. The first of these is a reinforcing and strengthening of the ego as it faces the outer world. Jung gave the name *persona* to this outward facing aspect. On the Roman theatrical stage actors wore their 'persona' – a mask to indicate the role they were playing. We can see it as protecting or defending the ego against the harsh demands of the super-ego. In our physical bodies the skin thickens to protect underlying tissues against outer pressure and the persona is a device with a similar function in the psyche. When the outer demands from the super-ego are harsh, or even fierce, reinforced by punishment, then the mask responds by developing armour to repel the attack. Reich designated this aspect 'character-armour' and showed what a barrier it could become, impermeable to both the super-ego from without and the id forces from within. By blocking the flow from the inner world and rejecting the influences of society, such a mask isolates the individual who lacks the influences he needs to bring him to maturity. Similarly the mask takes on the function of 'the idealized image of the self' which militates against change and development of the personality. It is as if at some stage a false adequacy has been attained and self-satisfaction hinders further growth to maturity.

The persona, however, need not be rigidly defending us from our neighbours. Its true function is that of relating to our neighbours. It is the means of contact through which we give out to our fellows – be they intimates or strangers – something of the wealth we ourselves are receiving from the inner life from the unconscious.

I take as an illustration the shop assistant. When we are unlucky we encounter someone who could not care less either for the customer or for the goods awaiting sale in the back-shop. No business is done that day. Contrariwise, we are greeted with a smile, a listening ear and an awareness that the shop is well-stocked and can in all probability supply our need. We observe the good relationships with both the outer and the inner world. The customer needs goods but the shop needs to let its materials reach society, be it the man on the street or the woman in her home. In commerce the goods stored in the warehouse have to be distributed to the retail shops and from these reach the community. A smiling shop assistant plays an important role in aiding distribution so that the flow of goods outward encourages the back-shop people to keep in good relationship with the warehouses and then business flourishes. Here the back-shop symbolizes the unconscious with its wealth of goods. The smiling shop assistant is the persona adequately relating to the outside world.

It is wise today for each of us to question – again and again – how we are relating to our neighbours and friends, asking whether the great wealth of the unconscious, its great resource, is using us as individuals to enrich the community in which we live.

This very down-to-earth homely illustration sheds light on an old well-tested saying, 'The more you give the more you get, such is the law of love.' We need to see ourselves as open channels, unblocked pipes taking from the infinite resource, holding it in our consciousness where it enriches our being, and giving it out again. Failure to give damages us in our humanity and deprives the folk in touch with us of what we have the potential to give them.

Another word about the persona – we must beware of identifying with it. However delightfully we smile and present ourselves to the world, let us keep in mind that there is the self behind the persona, the real man or woman behind the actor. Identification with the role impoverishes, while contact with the inner life – the unconscious – enriches, and one way of reminder is through the honesty of the dream. We cannot afford to deny the importance of what is given to us in our sleep.

The *censor* balances the persona on the left in our map, acting as a barrier to the flow of the id, the libido. Like the persona, the censor varies in its strength and permeability according in a large measure to the approvals and disapprovals in the child's early life. The dream evades the censor and brings into consciousness elements from the depth of our being which, as I have said, we cannot afford to deny. Here, in touch surely with the reality of spirit is the Self – the Vedic philosophers called it *atman* – and learning from them Jung teaches us that we must in our spiritual-analytic following discover this inner energy.

In the third chapter of the letter St Paul wrote to the Ephesians, he writes of 'the hidden self' attaching to this concept what Jung ascribes to the Self (*atman*). Paul says that it is through the Spirit (intuitive, non-intellectual awareness) that we discover the hidden self where he tells us 'Christ will live in our hearts through faith'. He thinks of this hidden self as 'planted in love and built on love' and teaches us that through this (let us recognize it as integral in everyman's psyche) we can grasp something of the dimensions of the Christ-love which can flow into our human lives. We then may become live wires to carry creative energy – with its loving, healing, renewing power – into the present day world. For as Paul says, 'This power working in us does infinitely more than we can ask or imagine.'

3.

The Light and the Dark: Yin and Yang

China, the land of ancient Eastern wisdom, is breaking into our Western consciousness all the more, it seems, with each year of our lives. In my youth there were many Christian missions to China but now China is sending the missionaries of her religion to us in the West. She has given us the great symbol of the Yin/Yang – the opposed yet combined interlocking sinuous shapes contained in the circle; the light with its 'eye' of darkness, the dark with the 'eye' of light. It has given us the *I Ching*, exploiting the philosophy of chance and only now are we Westerners accrediting the possibility that 'there is no such thing as accident'. Acupuncture, at one time derided in modern medicine, is proving its value with its possibilities of healing and wholeness. The beautiful, rhythmic, continuous movement of Tai-Ch'i makes nonsense of our dancing.

My patients and I dream often of China and Tibet and say we do not know why. The unconscious is the area of 'not knowing' and these dreams may be leading us into the deep, more than personal, unconscious, whence derives the intuitive wisdom that so enriches our days and our nights when it breaks through the barriers and floods our consciousness. These Eastern lands are antipodes far removed from Britain. We enter them only after a long journey and become aware of something there quite different lying on the opposite side of the globe. We remember that when it is day in China it is night in our country and that our daylight has left that country in darkness. We are dreaming, then, of opposites combined, since the same Sun and Moon illumine both.

Over the ages, the Sun and the Moon, light and dark, have been symbols of masculinity and femininity. The Sun, masculine, giving out and the Moon, feminine, receiving and reflecting. Freud developed this symbolism further. He saw in our dreams maleness represented by the dart, the spear, the sword, the needle, the fir-tree and the church spire. And he reminded us that the penis too is a symbol of manhood. Femininity in our dreams is symbolized by the containers, buckets, bottles, jars, boxes, boots, the child's cot, the spreading chestnut tree, the church itself, all symbolizing the womb – that in which things happen. Freud saw masculinity as that which penetrates, stirs to life, whereas femininity is patients and awaits the development of life within. But there is in each of us, men and women, both a Sun and a Moon, a giving out and a receiving. Just as the Sun gives light, so the Moon controls the tides. Each person must find the balance that holds true to their inner reality and does not come merely from the outer world of parents, peers and society.

Look again at the Yin/Yang symbol. Just as the Yin has her eye of brightness and the Yang his eye of darkness, so in the human psyche there is always the opposite waiting to be discovered. Yin/Yang is the symbol of wholeness. Yin does not cancel Yang but makes a wholeness with it. Life is full of these opposites and we are committed to the understanding that their co-existence is creative so long as the tension between them is observed. Life and Death – but what happens to man if Death takes a holiday? Joy and suffering – would life have meaning if there were no pain? Sunlight becomes tedious without cloud. Good and evil, who can guess their secret? An Old Testament question is, 'Shall there be evil in the city and the Lord hath not done it?'

The account of humanity's beginning in Genesis and also in the Atlantis myths seems to indicate an original androgeny, 'male and female created he them'. Only later were they separated into Adam and Eve, man and woman, male and female. Jung in his teaching has much to say on this subject and in what follows I am completely indebted to his inspiration. Jungian scholars may well find fault with my use of his material. It has been elaborated and curtailed and is not perhaps the orthodox teaching, but as I use it in my work day by day, it makes great sense and is helpful in the understanding of our problems.

Jung allots to each individual four possibilities of being, the four functions of life. They are intuition, sensation, feeling and thinking. Intuition is a purely spiritual function with no obvious physical instrument for its use. It is primitive, primordial, pre-human, extra-temporal. All living things, all beings, every cell, may be credited with this gift, this function, including the human zygote in the womb. It is a 'way of knowing' without as yet any organ through which it knows – with no brain, but with a mind, a psyche, capable of knowing. Its opposite, also primitive but now with some physical representation, is the sensory function. It operates through the five windows of perception, through which the outer reality is known to the individual – seeing, hearing, touching, smelling, tasting. It operates already in the womb, creating the organs through which later it receives impressions. Perhaps touching and hearing are the first developed, both before birth, ready to be used when the child, newly born, seeks and finds the breast. The hand represents the sensory function in the mnemonic we use to come to terms with this four-sidedness of the psyche: hunch, hand, heart, head.

Now the heart function – feeling. In the course of evolution, millions of years pass and with the development of parenthood a third function comes into being. Birds hatching their eggs keep in touch with their fledglings, both protecting and feeding them. Observing an ordinary domestic hen with her chicks we see qualities developing that were not there before she broods or in the intervals between brooding periods. First of all the anticipating patience, the sitting, the expectancy, qualities which later in evolution we can observe in woman. After the hatching the hen cares for her chicks, encourages them to feed, gathers them under her wings to protect and comfort them, so that we may think of her as the prototype of caring love. More than this, she develops a capacity for courage, attacking the enemy who would separate the chicks from her care, like the tigress with her cubs. In this creature, then, we see the development of the feeling function in its most primitive differentiation – into patience (i.e. waiting, expectation), caring, aggression, protection, all in some way *loving*.

Let us notice that whereas intuition and sensation seem to be inherently present in the cell, the unit of life, feeling is in the beginning dormant and needs to be elicited. It is the strong bond between parent and child that draws out from the offspring the capacity to love, to relate, to mate and to care for the children of the following generation. The rejected foundling, institutionalized from birth, has a poor chance of developing into the mature individual who can love his neighbour as he loves himself. There is, however, in all life the imponderable, the intervention of love from unknown sources, so that no one of us need despair that love can establish itself in our lives. We must ask, seek, knock, always with importunity and the gift, the experience of love will not be refused.

Let us notice also that many aspects of feeling are accompanied by – even recognized through – physical states. The two great counterbalanced emotions in human life are love and fear and we are aware of them through our bodies as well as through our states of mind. When love dominates, then we know ourselves to be loved and secure and we are therefore able to give love and comfort. We feel in harmony with life. When fear and anger become dominant, the music is jangled – life goes out of tune. To quote again what St Paul wrote to Timothy so long ago: 'God hath not given us the spirit of fear, but of power and of love and of the sound mind'. The 'spirit of fear' is anxiety, fear becoming master instead of servant. When fear is a habit, anxiety serves little useful purpose. Since God has not given us the spirit of fear, can we not live instead in the spirit of God, where power is energy, love is good relationships and the sound mind brings tranquillity.

Lastly, there is the thinking function. Descartes presumed that 'I think, therefore I am' and it is this dominance of thinking over the other three functions that is so great a problem in the West. Education stresses rational thinking to such an extent that in many cases we lose sight of our 'gut-reaction' when the body wants its say. When we come to believe only in rational thought and deny the validity of feeling, then tragedy develops.

Such repression of feeling may bring us into a situation where we are unable to feel, our hearts are hard, we scorn emotion. What has happened to us? Can we again get in touch with this lost quality?

Men as boys are brought up to repress their feelings, to keep a stiff upper lip, not to weep, to exercise control over their emotions which may be derided as womanly. Wartime demanded great repression of feeling. 'Don't allow yourself to consider, to feel who you are killing when the bombs are dropping, just get on with the business of war.' Have we yet recovered from the patterns imposed at that time? And what of the fate of women who in the past have so often been told not to bother developing their intellect, but instead to concentrate on being loving, gentle and comforting? Today we must be more and more conscious of what is happening, seeing this repression as a serious loss and not being content that it must be so, either for ourselves or for those who follow us. Many ways are opening through which the balance between the four functions can be restored. There are women's groups and now of late men's groups where we can begin to recover awareness of what is repressed.

As we regain this balance, there even appear to be changes in the patterns of electrical activity of the brain's hemispheres. Within recent years the fact that the brain consists of two hemispheres, a right and left connected by a bridge of nervous fibres called the *corpus callosum*, has been studied with renewed interest. There has been experimental work observing the damaged brains of epileptic patients as well as records made of the brain waves associated with different states of mind, of consciousness. Allowing for right- or left-handedness, it is now believed that the left hemisphere is predominantly 'interested' in material things, in the world of outer reality, physical environment, verbal and intellectual activity, business affairs and such like, while the other side concerns itself with spiritual values, with the world of inner reality, the intuitive, with religion, music, poetry and art. And it is of course uniting the two hemispheres that brings an enrichment to life.

Replacing now the squaredness of the four functions, let us add another dimension and create a sphere in rotation. The functions are all in contact and whatever the immediate situation, the apposite function presents itself. Everything is moving and as with Yin/Yang the opposites are united.

4.

The Unconscious

As human beings we pride ourselves on our highly developed consciousness. We are not only conscious – that is, aware – of our surroundings, but conscious of ourselves. 'Only man', it is said, 'knows that he knows'. By this extension of awareness we differentiate ourselves from all other animals. We share with them our anatomy, our senses, our energy and many of our innate behaviour patterns, but our capacity to 'look before and after and pine for what is not' seems to set us apart from all other living beings. Yet with the creatures too 'something is happening', consciousness is developing, and our relationship with them elicits what we have considered human qualities. Mammals that have returned to the ocean – seals and dolphins – startle us with their intelligence. Possibly this occurs because in the ocean they acquire a much greater freedom than the pedestrian mammals who keep their feet on the ground.

Since the word *unconscious* means literally *not knowing* it covers a wide variety of states: death, a drunken stupor, coma, the result of brain injury, sleep so profound that we 'sleep through' the noisy alarm clock. There is also a state between waking and sleeping when we see ridiculous impossible visions, and think irrational thoughts. Is there a background to consciousness always tending to break through? We make a great understatement when we use the illustration of the iceberg, saying that while one tenth is visible a further nine tenths are invisible: we cannot assess its unknown dimensions beneath the waters. We admit in our everyday talk the breakthrough of motivation from the unconscious, commonly, for instance, finding ourselves saying, 'I was quite unconscious of doing anything to hurt his feelings,' or, 'I was not conscious of doing anything helpful or praiseworthy,' or, 'I am forced to think ...,' or 'I can't help believing this though I know it is irrational.' In these cases, the word means literally 'not knowing.' Unconsciousness can also be the blindness of the lover, the floundering in emotion when reason fails us, the inability to understand what others find quite clear. There are endless moments in our lives when 'consciousness,' in this sense, fails us. Of course, once we realize that it has failed, we can say, 'I didn't know' and acknowledge that our ignorance is abysmal, but being unconscious of something also commonly involves being ignorant of one's own ignorance.

These are common, everyday meanings of the word, but in recent years the word 'unconscious mind' (or just 'the unconscious') has come into common use. The concept is now associated with the names of Freud and Jung: that there is a part of our mind of which we are not directly aware, but which is continually active, exerting dominant influence on our thoughts, our feelings and our behaviour, and perhaps most important of all on our health. The unconscious, when guilt-laden, can be seen as a cause of physical and mental illness, and access to it as the way of healing. The process of opening up and exploring what lies hidden in this area is called 'psychoanalysis' or 'analytical psychology.'

How does the unconscious manifest itself in our lives? The answer must be that all life is dependent on its activity. It is the Cosmos itself – the infinitely great Source – geared down, transformed, available for each of us. All art, music, drama, literature, all creativity – indeed life itself – has its source and origin in its depths. The German philosophers call it 'Urgrund' – ground of our being. Today we have learned how to be more aware of it and to get some notion of its working through dream analysis.

Dreams are one form of communication between the unconscious and conscious aspects of mind. They come to us in sleep when we are not 'conscious' yet we may remember them when we awake. Dreams use symbols of many kinds which need to be interpreted before we can understand their relevance. Symbols are, indeed, the language of the unconscious. Work on the physical accompaniments of dreaming has shown that babies dream long before they can talk. Do they dream perhaps in the womb? Mankind has recorded the fact of dreaming far back in history. Before the Jews became a people, Joseph influenced the fate of nations by his gift of interpretation. The Greeks accredited the origin of medical science to Asklepios, half god, half mortal, whose medical school at Epidauros attracted the sick from far and near, and their dreams were the vehicles of their healing. The relics which we can still see at Epidauros show that the invalids and injured were encouraged to use clay to represent their afflictions visually. We modern psychotherapists are using similar devices, encouraging patients to use paint or 'chthonic' material to represent their states of mind.

There are different *levels* of consciousness and numberless levels of the unconscious. Those of us, therapists as well as members of dream groups, and others who listen as people recount their dreams, are often confronted with the symbolism of the stairway, the ladder, the lift. The lift does curious things in dreams. Sometimes it shoots up through the roof, sometimes it halts between the landings, at other times it crushes us as we crouch in the lift-well. Sometimes its doors will not open; more usually, however, it serves its purpose and lands us on the level where we want to go. Stairs, similarly, present themselves as narrow or wide, as steep or gently sloping, as straight or curved or sometimes as diverging to right and left. Sometimes their bannisters are missing or we are aware of clinging on to them. Ladders are strange in dreams; rungs are broken and sometimes they seem to have no attachment above, though somehow (irrationally) they are supported at the top. And the levels we dream of? *Down* in the pit, the basement, the cellar – *up* in the attic or on the roof; ground level, first floor, second floor; *down* in the valley or river bed, *up* on the peak, the mountain top, the pinnacle – all these levels we enter in the dream world, they present different aspects of inner reality.

Dreams, called by Freud 'the royal road to the unconscious', are not the only means of communication with this aspect of our mind or psyche. As I have already said, there are things we say but take no full responsibility for saying. 'It just slipped out', we explain, or 'I could have bitten my tongue off', or 'I am so sorry, I didn't mean it.' In such cases we can profit by recognizing the truth, since in some deep sense we *did* mean it.

A more recent focus of interest as a source of communication with the unconscious is the question of *why we take ill*. Why do we catch germs, take influenza, break our bones, wrench our ligaments or muscles? Notice the active voice. In the language we use to talk about these illnesses and accidents we are *taking responsibility for what has happened.* 'I broke my leg', 'I hurt myself', 'I took pneumonia.' I once heard an old lady averring that she had 'stung herself with a bee'! The tummy-aches of the unwilling school child, the clergyman's sore throat, recurring unexplained 'temperatures,' accidents: is anything 'accidental'? These occurrences are all coming to be seen as attempts at communications from the unconscious – statements of unwillingness to enter creatively into life, or perhaps shoulder a burden that feels too heavy. It is important in such cases to ask not only *why* but *when* do these untoward symptoms occur? With some people they may, for instance, almost inevitably present themselves when all seems set for enjoyment.

Elizabeth, an acquaintance of mine, full of good works, seemed to have her life dogged by disaster. In her first love-affair the man died before their relationship came to fulfilment and subsequent love affairs were always with married men. She broke her leg on the eve of a mountain-climbing holiday; she took an infectious fever the day before she was due to join others on a trip abroad; she lost her voice on the very day she was due to give an important speech. Her friends came almost to count with certainty on such happenings and to ask: were they accidental? If her friends had insight they might also ask 'Why does she always need to punish herself on the eve of a pleasurable experience? Is she guilty? If so, about what?' She showed no evidence of conscious guilt, was indeed an extroverted, cheerful individual with a great involvement in caring for the under-dogs. The guilt was *unconscious* and to the end of her life she remained unaware of the deep need for punishments she inflicted on herself (and incidentally on others) through ill-health. Even retirement brought suffering instead of a happy old age.

What is the source of all these communications? Why does the unconscious send them? What does it contain? The answer given by the analysts is that the personal unconscious – the cellar, Freud's symbolic word – contains disapproved, rejected, or repressed material – memories and feelings so painful that they could not be tolerated by the conscious mind and were pushed down into the 'cellar'. Dreams often contain symbols of a cellar, a basement, a junk shop, a deep hole, a black pit. From this body of repressed material, preserved exactly in the condition in which it was banished, issue not only dreams, slips of the tongue, and physical distress, but also fear, anxiety, phobias, and disturbed or compulsive behaviour. Moreover, things are not inactive and peaceful in the cellar: the repressed material is held down only by a great expenditure of energy. Not only is the life-stream dammed up and unavailable for the work of daily life, but its energy is being used to maintain repression in a totally unproductive way.

The picture is rather like this – some adults are preoccupied in some serious affair in a large house. They are constantly interrupted and distracted by noisy young children. Unable to tolerate these frustrating distractions, they take the children one by one, down the stairs to the cellar. The door is closed on them, and all is quiet. Now oblivious to the children the grown-ups can complacently pursue their important work – but not for long. The cellar contains the control to the house, the gas mains, the electric fuse box, and the main water shut off. Active children, discovering new power in their hands, have a good time turning off the mains. Soon the folk upstairs are shivering with cold and frustrated in the absence of their services. There is nothing for it but to go down into the cellar, find out what is happening and deal with the emergency. The moral is that repression cuts off the power, the psychic energy, which is essential to mature creativity.

We cannot afford to disregard the cellar, this area of rejected instinctual activity. Entering it, through analysis or therapy, we are able to restart the flow of the libido, the life-forces, which bring into our lives insight and understanding, the warmth and comfort of good relationships and the tranquillity that comes when our frustrations lessen or disappear.

Beneath the cellar and beyond our personal unconscious lie greater depths for exploration where we can contact the feeling of our fellow mortals and also, it may be, the wisdom of the ages reaching down to the Source of our being. Sometimes I hear it argued that only foolish people would go down into the unconscious – that is, undertake some form of self-knowing; but I would urge everyone not to hesitate to open the door to the cellar, and to descend the steps carefully with a guide if there is still darkness there, for the reward will be great. The discovery of all its lost but valuable materials will give access to energy and understanding previously unimagined. Robert Browning, taking up Christ's teaching in which the hidden wisdom is likened to a pearl of great price, writes in his poem *Paracelsus*:

> Are there not
> Two points in the adventure of the diver
> One – when, a beggar, he prepares to plunge,
> One – when, a prince, he rises with his pearl?

Worthwhile? Yes, infinitely worthwhile. Today, as well as the methods of traditional analysis, there are a number of other ways in which people can be helped to come to terms with the past, buried in their unconscious. Instruction is available in deep meditation and in the practice of Yoga, as well as in a legion of group activities. All of these tend to break down the barriers in ourselves between conscious and unconscious, so that we have a better understanding of similar problems in our neighbours, and become better parents, teachers or employers.

Teilhard de Chardin in his book *The Phenomenon of Man* deals with the evolution of consciousness. In the beginning is energy. He calls it 'the sub-atomic dust.' Energy and matter are almost indistinguishable at this stage of evolution but gradually matter emerges. He talks of the 'lithosphere' – literally the realm of the stones. We know it as the inorganic, pre-living world. Something happens and we find the crystals forming which have marvellous structures as if a rhythm has been imposed on matter – a rhythm which creates beauty.

Now more is happening: life, the biosphere, the tree of life takes root and begins to grow. In its beginning the vegetable and animal worlds are indistinguishable and of no size at all, only visible through a microscope. In the course of aeons – time out of mind – the two stems separate like great trees each branching, each differentiating as it grows, till we have the animal and vegetable kingdom linked, interdependent, each still evolving, it must be, towards a goal, *still unconscious*. Alpha is the beginning, Omega ahead of us beckons us on towards fulfilment. Human life is a brief consciousness between the great Unknowns. Mortal man as he lives in his body knows certainly that he must die, but also has a certainty that the flame which is his spirit will always be lit again in the great flame of God's Presence.

Let us hold fast to the comforting assurance:

I am spirit. I have a body.

I shall look at this idea again in a later chapter.

5.

Repression and Analysis

The word *repression*, the idea of the repressed personality (in colloquial language a buttoned-up person), and even the phrase 'the return of the repressed' are common-place in speech and writing today. But the meaning of repression as understood by the analyst, its great significance and the phenomenon of the re-emergence of repressed material are matters well worth reconsidering and understanding.

To be accepted is pleasurable: to be rejected is painful. These processes of acceptance or rejection begin early in life, operating already in the young infant whose psyche is plastic and vulnerable, sensitive to disapproval which he tends to avoid. Even in the ante-natal days 'the pregnancy' is either accepted with joy or rejected with dismay.

The good baby, accepted by the mother, lives in a pleasant atmosphere of peace and serenity, while the naughty child, also designated 'bad' or 'difficult' finds life extremely unpleasant. To make matters easier for himself he may discard the disapproved behaviour, accepting the values of his disapproving parents which now dictate how he reacts to his environment. If he decides to be 'good' it is at great cost. All too often what he discards is vital to his well-being and to his creativity, and when repressed it is no longer available. He has lost, we say, his aggression. 'I want' is no longer on his lips from dawn to dusk since he has accepted the 'you ought' of his parents, now operating as 'I ought.' We find him good, obedient, easily managed (shall we say manipulated) now acceptable to teachers, authorities, the bosses whom he is willing to serve without resentment or anger. He seems to be quite unconscious of what he has lost – shall we say it is 'lost in the unconscious'. He is bereft of some virtue as if the steel rod of the backbone has become flaccid and no longer holds him erect.

The vitality and strength of will which was his birthright are no longer available. He lacks aggression and with it initiative and creativity. If Scottish, he is called a douce lad, implying that he follows rather than leads, submits rather than makes a fuss, is a good servant but lacks the initiative to be a good master.

The birthright of each of us as human beings, or indeed as belonging to the animal kingdom, is that we have at our disposal psychic energy which motivates our lives. It operates through the instincts, coming into awareness as *I want*. I want to know, I want to eat and drink, I want to find a mate. The wanting of the libido – we use the word to denote the flow of energy in each life – differentiates itself until in the end, maybe, it becomes 'I want to die' as we see that we want nothing more of life.

Repression does not take place once and for all: it continues to act throughout our lives. It is not only a mental process, but one in which the total body musculature participates. When we are tense the muscle fibres go into spasms or 'knots' so that skilled massaging fingers detect them as fibrositis nodules which disappear as the muscle relaxes. What does this involve but an expenditure of energy, no longer directed outwards towards the world and its need, but inward, pushing back the life-forces, rendering the muscles painful and inoperative? We can see here two different aspects of the listless, in-valid, asthenic sufferer. His psychic energy is imprisoned and unavailable; but also, as I have just said, the energy used to imprison his vitality is not free to keep the wheels of his life turning. By analogy we might say this is a double loss to society – the prisoner and the gaoler are both out of action. Think of the immense cost of keeping the prisoner in prison!

Some of these sufferers – our neurotic patients – remain repressed throughout their lives and never fulfil their potential. Not only this; but in their invalidism they absorb the energy of others – devoted daughters, heroic sons, and the innumerable individuals staffing our hospitals which care for the sick, the psychotic, the invalids, the prematurely old.

In very many cases, however, there is a break-through. The repression weakens through age, change in community standards or other factors, and the behaviour alters often dramatically. Alcohol and drugs may have this effect temporarily, so that the person under their influence is unrecognisable to himself or others. The repressed material is no longer under control and the disapproved behaviour, so well locked away for years, again emerges. This is 'the return of the repressed'.

Think of the army officer – a colonel approaching middle age. He has been disciplined all his life – from his earliest years through public school onwards – and his job has involved the discipline of his subordinates. Now, however, the repressing forces are weakening and he finds himself at the mercy of uncontrollable rages, strangely similar to the infantile tantrums for which his nanny smacked his bottom in his nursery years! Again look at the dignified reserved man of letters, a professor perhaps by now. At a party where alcohol is flowing freely he may be found making improper suggestions or very unsuitable advances to ladies with whom he has only a limited acquaintance. When the process of repression returns next day he has 'forgotten' all about it.

Similarly, dear old ladies who have 'guarded their lips and never allowed themselves bad language' may find themselves – unaccountably and very distressingly – damning the Almighty or having 'very ugly words' coming to mind when they pray – an 'unforgivable sin'. Probably they had long ago picked up a swearword at school or from their brothers, had been penalised and told 'Never let me hear you use such words again.' These are all instances of rejected material escaping the control of the super-ego, bringing distress to the individual whose idealised image of himself still persists. Now 'the ice is melting', that is, the repressing forces are weakening and out come these naughty words, unchanged from that day of punishment and repression. It is, of course, the aim of the analyst to liberate the valuable energy and the long-forgotten creativity of the person under analysis. To do this he allows the patient to *transfer* on to him the feelings originally held towards his parents, his brothers and sisters, his school-masters – in fact any, or in turn all of the 'dramatis personae' of his early years. It is this 'transference' which enables the analysis to proceed and the analyst's skill consists in establishing, analysing and ultimately rejecting the projections which it contains. That is what makes analysis so long and often so painful a process, expensive in every way to both parties concerned.

Fear is the major element in repression, often plainly fear of punishment. I remember a woman who recalled with bitterness what she called a 'belting' in early childhood. 'Did your mother often belt you?' I asked. 'No, no,' she answered, 'a look in her face was enough ever afterwards.' I think this case may explain the problem of the patient who is 'quite sure her parents never punished her' but has all her life been so good and obedient that it was unnecessary. She has repressed the incident since it seemed so out of character with the loving parent. The most loving parents, however, have their off-days; exasperated beyond belief they 'could murder that child.' This child, good and obedient beyond belief, may suffer during a long life from this one incident, reinforced subsequently only by a disapproving look on the mother's face.

Had the tantrums of the child been dealt with adequately the child would have learned to cope with his rages: the emotion would have gradually become valuable and of service instead of destructive and somewhat ridiculous in later life. Repression is of course a necessary disciplining and civilizing force in life; but it can be used gently, not fiercely. The instinctual energy must *flow*, not escape volcanically and inappropriately as it tends to do if the repressing forces are harsh and unduly restrictive.

Jerry, a man in his fifties, has come for treatment because of his inability to stand up for himself with his colleagues or even his subordinates. *He is afraid they will be angry* if he insists on carrying out his own ideas of which they disapprove. He recollected an occasion, he thinks he was four years old, when he was very angry with his mother and made a scene. She told him to go and stand in a dark passage until he was sorry. She seemed to be very angry with him and he felt desperately alienated from her and afraid. To his great surprise his father appeared and spoke to him gently, comforting him and even took him out and gave him an ice-cream. He found this very surprising at the time and believes that it was unusual for his father to go against his mother's rulings and that this was an isolated incident. It seemed that her domination was accepted and taken for granted in the family. The thought of opposing her and arousing her anger was terrifying. Safety lay in being good, that is in rejecting his own anger until in time it was not available, 'put away in deep freeze', repressed.

At this point in his analysis there was some evidence that it was not dead, only in 'deep freeze,' and slight signs of its availability were showing. Now the ice-cream incident seemed important, so that he could contemplate at least the *possibility* that anger had positive value and might earn approval from other men. Quite soon after this he dreamt that he lived in a great house as its master, but he went down to the basement to a servants' hall and was dancing with the servants. Anger, sex, curiosity, acquisitiveness and all the instincts which we share with the other creatures are (like fire) good servants but bad masters. His dream indicates that he was coming to terms with his instinctual life in the unconscious – so often in dreams symbolised by the basement.

When the release of repressed instinctual energy first occurs it is frequently accompanied by guilt and fear. Repression took place long ago because the action or the word or the feeling was adjudged *bad*, therefore it was put away and became forgotten *with a quota of guilt to ensure the efficacy of the repression* – much as the sailors weighted the corpse with a cannon ball to ensure it stayed at the bottom of the sea. Dreams at this juncture may indicate how unacceptable the material is, and how guilty the dreamer still feels; for example: 'Four dark men burst open the door and came in. They were unwashed and the stink of their bodies was almost unbearable.'

In the dream groups, quite often non-attendance of a member is subsequently explained by the fact that dreams indicating his homosexuality or other guilty, unacceptable material are occurring and he fears that they will be disapproved. Dreams about defaecation fail to be contributed till the leader sees the difficulty and suggests, 'Let's just call it shit.' This brings a great release of tension with laughter and a plethora of shitting dreams for a season! Similarly, the group's attention in the earlier case is usually turned to the common, perhaps universal, problem of men – that of homosexuality at some stage in their lives, but not necessarily labelled 'gay' or 'queer', and of women whose lesbianism tends to be denied, although the first of all relationships, that of mother and daughter, can always be re-awakened.

The real joy of analysis, with the return of the repressed material, for both analyst and analysed person is the emergence of hidden gifts. 'Unmusical' patients discover they can sing or they acquire a musical instrument and develop abilities which bring great pleasure to themselves and others. 'Inartistic' folk begin to paint and get prizes for poster-painting or have their work exhibited and noticed by critics. Dull people find themselves witty; stupid people take delight in study. A gift for poetry often emerges: others previously inarticulate find a gift for public speaking. Best of all, perhaps, some for long unloved and unloving discover that their power of love is not dead, only frozen. Ice melts and the sweet water flows again through them into other people's lives. They have discovered the hidden self so long unknown, the creative virtue which is every man's birthright, the Christ in their lives who makes all things new.

Analysis may be a long journey, cost every penny we can find, be fraught with many set-backs, but it is always worthwhile. The more we give of our guilt-laden experience, the more we get out of the enduring creative treasure. Such is the law of love and of the analytic process.

So let us again allow ourselves to know that we are the recipients of psychic energy. St Paul (Jerusalem Bible translation) says that we are earthenware jars to hold the treasure – the treasure being the energy, the virtue, the quota of creativity each individual is given, given for his own growth and development but given in order that he may serve the creative purpose. Unused (like the talent buried in the earth) it sends us to hell: that is, it causes us pain and suffering and we drag others with us. Make use of your gifts and they will multiply. You will get mastery over the environment and become, in the words of the parable, ruler over ten cities.

6.

The Wound and its Healing

When we put our minds to the further understanding of healing and the process of 'getting better' it brings us to the awareness that in the course of life the wound, the *trauma*, is inevitable. Birth must bring great separation-anxiety to the new-born, with the shock of physical change from darkness, warmth, containedness and the re-assuring sound of the mother's heart-beat into a chilly world, all too brightly lit for the eyes' comfort.

Not only human life but all life begins with a wounding. The bee wounds the flower in the act of pollination, and the man the woman in the primal act of intercourse. The babe wounds the mother as he opens her body for his birth. Vulnerable, all of us, we are subject to the wounds of everyday life in body and in spirit.

Wounding is a two-way process of inflicting and receiving – no one escapes. Unconscious processes are often at work. 'I didn't mean to', we say, when we realize how wounding our words or our actions have been. There is an inevitability about wounding, even in a love relationship, where it can cause a 'sweet pain' which is acceptable and not merely tolerable, opening up a level of life-experience hitherto untouched. This is emphasized in the New Testament teaching that all suffering bears fruit.

We may think then, in the first place, of the parent-child interaction, and question whether this relationship ever escapes mutual wounding. Already we have considered the postulate of the father-mother-child inter-relatedness as a wounding situation, causing resentment and suffering in spite of love and care. A wound of the body that is tolerated heals quickly, but if it is open to constant re-stimulation of hurt it cannot heal. So with the wounds of the spirit – of the psyche. It is needless and unwise to increase the suffering by resentment: rather 'let be' – it will heal.

But can children tolerate the wounds of the punishing or unloving parent without resentment? I doubt it. Whenever a small child is smacked, hit, hurt by the parent's disapproval, he must want to hit back. This, however, is not likely to be allowed, and the wish to hit back remains in the unconscious, to be re-awakened later. Hence the subdued child may become the aggressive angry teenager. Parents must seek for ways of understanding rather than of punishing, since punishing inevitably creates resentment and ill-will. Society itself must face this question. Do we punish the criminal, in so doing increasing his hostility, or are there therapeutic methods, methods of mutual understanding through which release will come? 'Tout comprendre est tout pardonner' says the French proverb: to understand all is to forgive all.

A great revolution is needed in persuading 'the powers that be' politicians, sociologists, social workers, psychiatrists, magistrates, and parents that the structure of the family, the original triangle, the *trigone* of trigonometry on which architecture is based, is all important. It is here – in the strength or weakness of family security that the great percentage of problems lie which cause the violence, destructiveness, vandalism, lovelessness, bitterness and class-warfare in today's world.

Research work done in the U.S.A. on the higher apes demonstrates unquestionably that insufficient mothering devastates the chances of the off-spring coming to maturity, and, in turn, being adequate parents. The world's parents, in every country, in every rank of life, aristocrats as well as the un-housed, all need to grasp these inescapable truths. Let us look them squarely in the face, visualizing clearly what unloving parents are doing to their children and therefore to the world. Prison reform is obviously a great necessity at this moment but we must go further back, more deeply into the problem, and ask, 'Who are these prisoners – these criminals?' What we call 'depth-psychology' always inevitably leads us back into the parent-child relationship and its part in determining the spiritual health of the oncoming generations. Analysts should be *shouting* at the politicians asking them to see where, at what depth in human life, the wound is a running sore.

Trips to the moon and beyond have absorbed enormous energy, time, money and interest. Can we possibly bring ourselves to abandon the outer things in order to shed light on the basis of human life, which is love? Are our children's lives 'planted in love and built on love' so that from them again vigorous life will spring and develop?

Lack of love at conception, rejection during pregnancy, the uncaring reception of the new-born, breast denial, unacknowledged paternity, lack of the home, institutions replacing families, deprived unhappy children – what handicaps are we laying upon them in their struggle towards adult usefulness and maturity? Again and again we must return to the role of the individual since 'society' is only a concept that has strange unreality. The individual as channel – or even as 'earthenware jar to hold the treasure' – may be very small or even insignificant. But the treasure is the seed, and when it is nurtured in the good earth it will bear its corn, its fruit, quite beyond our reckoning or imagining.

The image of the *nest* thrusts itself into my mind as I write – so clear a symbol of parental care. The nest must be built before the eggs are laid and must be kept intact till the fledglings can desert it because of their strength. Broken homes are like abandoned nests. What is happening to the fledglings?

There is a further unhappy consequence to the infliction of wounds within the family. Parent-inflicted wounds are likely to lead to self-inflicted wounds. We may find ourselves and others accident-prone, subject to recurring illness, somehow intolerant of good health. We must ask whether so much of this injury, which we attribute to accident, is not self-inflicted – a need to punish ourselves because of our unconscious guilt.

Experiences with people outside our immediate family can

also be hurtful. Sometimes a wound can seem inflicted particularly on that part of ourselves with which we face the outside world – the 'persona' or mask. Once in my own experience an example of this wound to the persona occurred when I resented a broken appointment. A stranger had phoned in to ask for my help, in her distress, and at some cost and inconvenience to myself I had arranged an appointment. She did not come at the time we had arranged and it later transpired that she had found someone better-esteemed to visit! I felt *resentful* and invalidated, with an accompanying depression and loss of energy. Suddenly, as I brooded on the situation, I realized that it was my self-importance that was suffering. My pride was wounded, the false pride of the mask, vulnerable to the attack of society. I knew that there was a more real *self*, protected because it lay deep in the psyche (in religious terms it was 'in God's keeping'), the hidden self which cannot be damaged by insult, nor invalidated by lack of esteem. In psychological imagery we place it in touch with the unconscious as if the shadow has moved or faded to make room for it.

Many such incidents occur in the course of a professional career. They hurt because the face we present to the world – the persona – is fragile and vulnerable, and exposes itself to injury. Maturity, however, can develop and a strengthening of the real self through awareness that 'I' matter less and less, that there is a 'Not I' available, the unconscious resource, on which we increasingly learn to depend. This maturity wins the day, 'ripeness is all', and we see such incidents and all rebuffs as purely accidental and no longer able to wound us. The strong mature inner self needs no mask; it can afford to let the persona diminish, become transparent and fade away, coinciding with the break up of the 'shadow' in the personal unconscious.

What does this mean in everyday living? Perhaps a getting away from our egocentricity, a realization that life is like that, that we are all very ordinary people and must expect some hurt in the rough and tumble of life; perhaps laughing at our self-importance, understanding one more facet of human nature.

A verse comes to mind, published anonymously in *The Times* in 1916, a period in which a slogan 'It all depends on you' was on every hoarding because of war-time need to mobilize all resources. It read thus:

It all depends on me, a nobody,
If nobody I can and dare to be,
Effaced of self, dependent on the All,
Invulnerable though the heavens fall.

One of the most striking examples of a wound which results in healing is that inflicted in surgery. On occasion, how thankful we are that surgeons are available to open up the abscess when the tension causes agony, to remove the cancer which otherwise destroys the body. Surgeons may wound the skin and flesh in order to unite the broken bone. Nowadays, more than ever in the past, do they operate– with a preliminary wounding, an opening up– to repair and reconstitute the functioning of our organs. In the psyche, too, we must allow the infliction of the wound which comes with self-knowledge and the shattering of the mask. We must pray for a gentle therapist, but not avoid the necessity of letting go of our 'idealized images', be they of parent, lover or friend or – even more importantly – of ourselves, clinging to the idea of our own goodness and righteousness.

Parents are particularly vulnerable to the brick-bats of their adolescent children. At puberty the sexual hormones reinforce the body growth but also give the psyche renewed individual energy. The growing teenagers assert their equality with the parents or even their superiority and acquire courage to face the 'parental aggression'. It is a period of great importance to both parent and off-spring in which it is right that neither dominates and destroys but that through giving and taking, through sharing, through understanding opposing points of view, the spirit of equality develops. It may be that just in the measure that the parent has inflicted pain through punishment, the adolescent will now need to retaliate with his wounding words and deeds. In the tolerant receptive parents the wounds will heal, the arrogant self righteous parents are equally wounded but their lack of understanding prevents the healing and they cannot forgive. *Again* 'To understand all is to forgive all'; to forgive and be forgiven brings the healing of the wound.

The *renunciation* of physical superior strength is at this time forced upon the parent as the child grows to his adult stature. He has to admit the fact of bodily equality. When his desire to see his offspring mature predominates the parent renounces his need to know best, to be in the right, to acknowledge his mistaken ideas, then and only then can good relationships be established and kept.

There are some wounds which do not heal – running sores, that keep us humble. In the early story of Jacob wrestling with the angel, in which Jacob's thigh was dislocated – we are told that he went lame to the end of his life. In spite of this he emerges from the fight as a prince, a wounded prince. It may be that for some of us the unhealed wound is a necessity, so that we may be humble and learn more fully, that is from ever deeper levels, to understand the mysteries of the psychic processes.

Oedipus – adopted by Freud as hero – had also a wounded foot. Abandoned by his parents, exposed and pegged down on the hilltop, he bore the stigma of this wound all his life. The word 'Oedipus' actually means 'the swollen foot'. Equally cruel wounds led to his blindness in middle life. What Freud called in the first place 'the Oedipus complex' is now referred to as 'the Oedipus situation' in acceptance of the fact that the father-mother-son love-hate relationship is inherent in every family, carrying with it inevitable suffering and guilt. So Jacob wrestling with the angel before he crossed the ford Jabok, and Oedipus slaying his father at the cross roads – both of these locations symbolize the human faculty of choice, of decision-making, both inflict upon their heroes the wound that marks them for life. As human beings we wound and are wounded, but as spiritual beings – the children of the Most High – we know that His will for us is healing and redemption, that is, 'All things new'.

I am fairly sure that Robert Browning never heard about Freud, psychoanalysis, or 'the unconscious' but he has written beautifully about it with the imagery of the pearl-diver. I have quoted it already but here it is again:

> Two points in the adventure of the diver
> One – when, a beggar, he prepares to plunge,
> One – when, a prince, he rises with his pearl.

Interpreting, we say: The unconscious is the ocean. The pearl is the self – 'of great price.' It takes great courage to plunge into the unconscious, but as beggars we have great need. As princes we emerge, now in possession of the deeply-hidden treasure: the self has come into consciousness and its value is determined in the market place. To the world of men and women precious truth has been given by the courageous seeker after wisdom.

T.S. Eliot did know a lot about Freud and psycho-analysis and the unconscious. He writes:

> The wounded surgeon plies the steel
> And questions the distempered part.
> Beneath his bleeding hands we feel
> The cool dispassion of the healing art.

Interpreting this we would say, 'Discover your own wounds, your own shame, your own poverty and alienation. Then, and only then, set out to do the healing work of psychotherapy.' The therapist – the one who shares – has acquired, through the consciousness of his own dark, disreputable aspect, the ability to bring his patient into the milieu of healing. He has plunged like a beggar and emerged as a prince.

7.

'My Illness': The Interdependence of Body and Spirit

Do we – either as doctors or patients – fully understand the experience which we talk of as psychosomatic illness? Do we get the sense of unity of soul and body – their *synergy*? Is there any possibility that in pain and suffering we are doing our best to separate them? We say 'purely physical,' 'obviously psychological.' Browning writes'Not soul helps body more than body soul', and the same might be said of their mutual destructiveness when their unity is denied.

An old Scotsman, suffering from heart pains diagnosed as 'pseudo-angina', and at odds with the doctors, used to say to me: 'They tell me there's naethin' the matter, Doactor, but Ah tell ye Ah'm deein.' Is there something seriously 'the matter' with these physicians who do not understand that when someone is 'ill' something *is* the matter, whether they are able to diagnose it or not? Increasingly let all of us be humble and seek for more light, more understanding, more awareness. It may even have to come through our own illness.

When we listen to people talking about their ill-health – and this is a subject very dear to some – we may notice a certain proprietary quality – *my* headaches, *my* cough, *my* skin troubles, *my* bad leg, *my* troublesome indigestion and so on. Some time ago I too was afflicted with what I notice I am still apt to call 'my illness.' I shall return to it later.

Other people's illnesses may be tiresome to a listener; but to me, since I am a therapist, they must be interesting. I must ask myself: What are people trying to express with their symptoms? Is it possible that these are bodily, outer evidences of an inner psychic or spiritual disease? Another question arises too. Why has this illness come on *now*? The timing of onset may be all-important to its understanding and healing.

My patients will quite probably produce an outer, physical cause; and indeed these are important, since psyche and physique, spirit and body, maintain a partnership to be acknowledged and respected. Such causes can include the terribly cold weather, the damp climate, in summer the dust that is blown around, indigestible food, accident, allergy. Some patients, however, endowed with insight, will be conscious of *tension* as an underlying cause. They will mention things like a too protracted visit from a wife's or husband's relatives, undone tasks provoking guilt, grief over bereavement, anxiety over a child's illness or an adolescent's behaviour. Legion indeed are such factors which are listed as 'psychological' but underlying them all is tension. For instance, tense muscles give rise to a condition known as fibrositis or muscular rheumatism. The knotted muscle fibres are felt as nodules, but they disappear when relaxation occurs under the skilled hand of the masseur. Resentful people are often tense, too tense for comfort, and their joints suffer, although they quite probably are unaware of the tension. Psychological literature replaces the word resentment by 'repressed hostility' and lists it as a predisposing cause, or even in some cases the exciting cause, of rheumatic illness in its all too common manifestations today. Tension in the muscles of the neck and scalp give rise to headaches and, all through the systems of the body we can find similar tightness causing pain and other disturbances of function.

Children faced with uncongenial work at school, or with situations they wish to avoid, are often laid low with tummy pains, headaches, even a temperature, which enables them to escape the unwelcome or dreaded occasion. Often no physical cause can be found. Pain is subjective; no-one but the sufferer can assess its severity, but it is real enough, even though the causation may be suspect.

'My illness' is never accidental. Let us think of it further as a *mode of communication*: the unconscious aspect of our life talking to us. Can we listen and try to understand?

> It may be saying: 'I am no one's child. I need to be cared for. Can I attract attention or even love?' Illness takes us back to the situation in childhood and infancy when we could *demand* attention; someone had to care, we had a sort of omnipotence, we would die unless we were cared for.

> But 'our illness' may be telling us something rather different. It may be confronting us with the fact that our life is too full, we are too busy, we have 'no time' for what needs to be done. Our illness forces us to take time to *be*, not only to *do*.

> It may be forcing us into a better understanding of other people. It is easy for strong healthy people to be scornful of the weaklings and their illnesses, but now sympathy is almost extorted from us as we become aware of our own weaknesses.

These are some of the differing needs that force illness upon us and individuals find individual reasons. What is important is to try to *understand the motivation*, to ask: *why* am I ill and *why* just at this time? The answer may be slow to come and the illness resistant to cure, but the cure may not be of ultimate importance. The illness has its own function in our life and in the life of the family. Grasping its purpose, comprehending its apparent necessity in the here and now, understanding more as a fresh viewpoint is accepted, all these bring an increase of the potential life-energy and the ability to *create* the environment rather than be dominated by it.

'My illness,' therefore, may have positive value. Out of it further understanding of life can emerge. We can quite truthfully talk of 'the *need to fall ill!*' Perhaps too quick a 'cure' may actually lead to further trouble, a switch over to alternative symptoms. Better, maybe, to wait with patience for the understanding that will result in healing. Surgeons tell us that wounds must heal from the bottom, so in our illnesses, instead of demanding *cure* we have often to wait for *healing* from the deep unconscious.

I have already mentioned that there are cases where 'my illness' may be so precious and valuable to me that I am reluctant to let it go. The weekly visit to the doctor's surgery, or the recurring admission to the 'skin ward' of the hospital, supply in some cases the only times when interest and sympathy are available. Can they be lightly abandoned? The cure of a physical disease may precipitate emotional illness such as depression. It seems that the unconscious aspect of the psyche prefers physical illness to states in which we are unhappy and feel ourselves worthless. To illustrate this I shall tell you of the very first patient whom I treated by analytic therapy, that is by listening and trying to understand without prescribing drugs or other physical treatment.

Chrissie was in her late twenties and had never been well. She came complaining of dyspnoea (breathlessness) which came on with any exertion so that she was virtually a prisoner in the home. She came supported on the arm of an older sister who had also been imprisoned by her devotion to the invalid. I listened as she recounted her dreams and also to her memory of early incidents in life. Her mother later became interested and supplied this story.

An attack of whooping-cough coincided with the birth of a brother when Chrissie was two years old. There was a dramatic scene – the nurse, calling at the house to attend to the mother and the new baby, had her attention drawn to Chrissie with a blue face, choking in a paroxysm of coughing. 'I fear she is a gonner' were the words preserved through the years as she picked up Chrissie and put her on the mother's lap, where she found herself again an object of compassion and interest, usurping the place of the new baby. All these years later the drama was being relived with recurring attacks of dyspnoea. She reported 'I go black in the face and the neighbours come in to see me die.'

I had only seen Chrissie a few times when this whooping-cough story was elicited. She did *not* remember the incident but her mother told her of it. The effect was extremely drastic. *Chrissie lost her illness.* She could move freely, and come unattended to the clinic without dyspnoea. I had to leave

London at that juncture for two weeks and when I returned was greeted with a terrible story. Chrissie was now in a state of deep depression, threatening suicide. My reaction was interesting – I felt very guilty. I had deprived Chrissie of her all-important symptom which reinstated her as a centre of interest, a very important suffering invalid. What had I done?

We had a long way to go together finding causes which had reinforced the pattern, including early sexual involvements which said 'Withdraw ... Sex is dangerous ...You are safer as an invalid ... Your illness has value – it reinstates you in the centre of the picture, an object of sympathy and compassion – it is dangerous to relinquish the symptoms.'

I am glad to relate that this patient had *the courage to get well*, worked through her depression and quite soon had found a job and was a relatively independent woman for the first time in her life.

Discretion on the part of the therapist and courage on the part of the patient are both necessary in dealing with chronic sickness. The understanding of its causation must be linked in the patient's mind with a sense of forgiveness *(tout comprendre est tout pardonner)* and only with this can the wound be truly healed. Let us remember how Christ said: 'Son, thy sins are forgiven thee' *before* he said 'Take up they bed and walk.'

Edward Carpenter in his book *Towards Democracy* has a short poem which deals most wisely with this relationship between the body and the psyche. It is called 'Stupid Old Body' and in it he likens the body to the dog in his master's care. He has written:

> Do not pay too much attention to the stupid old body.
> When you have trained it, made it healthy, beautiful, and your willing servant,
> Why, do not then reverse the order and become its slave and attendant.
> (The dog must follow its master – not the master the dog)
> Remember that if you walk away from it and leave it behind, it will have to follow you – it will grow by following, by continually reaching up to you.
> Incredibly beautiful it will become, and suffused by a kind of intelligence.
> But if you turn and wait upon it – and its mouth and its

belly and its sex-wants and all its little ape-tricks –
preparing and dishing up pleasures and satisfactions for these,
Why then, instead of the body becoming like you, you will become like the body,
Incredibly stupid and unformed – going back in the path of evolution – you too with fish-mouth and toad-belly, and imprisoned in your members,
As it were an Ariel in a blundering Caliban.

Therefore quite lightly and decisively at each turning point in the path leave your body behind –
With its hungers and sleeps, and funny little needs and vanities – paying no attention to them;
Slipping out at least a few steps in advance, till it catches you up again,
Absolutely determined not to be finally bound or weighted down by it.
Or fossilized into one set form –
Which alone after all is Death.

As a child I remember hearing the Border shepherds admonishing their collies. 'Come in ahint' they would shout. Carpenter is there reminding us of the shepherd's orders to the creature who serves him and his flock: '*Come in ahint*– Come to heel.' The dog must follow the master, not the master the dog.

And now I want to look at 'my illness' in my own life. *I fell ill* on 15th July 1977. I had done a day's work with patients and was standing at the window reading a paper when I fell helpless on the floor. I had not lost consciousness, could move my toes and fingers and could speak, so reassured myself that it was not a cerebral disaster. The doctors said later it was an acute virus infection of the labyrinth, that part of the anatomy of the ear which enables us to maintain balance. Others might have attributed it to an attack by the evil one. One wise patient interested in the involvement of the labyrinth, was sure it had to do with me as Ariadne in league with my patients in the defeat of the Minotaur!

After some weeks of almost complete prostration I staggered

back into activity. I found patients unwilling to be deserted, so adopting the conviction of St Paul, 'I can do all things through Christ which strengtheneth me' and the many Old Testament exhortations to be of good courage, I found myself active again with energy for analysis, for writing, for dream group therapy and even for speaking acceptably to larger audiences. In a measure, energy seemed to flow according to the demand made.

Over three years later, I am still unsteady, limited in my physical outgoings, questioning my ability to recover completely. As I write 'recover' I ask myself: what does this mean? Do I want to 'recover' or is the apposite word 'Do I want to 'get better'?' – to occupy, it may be, new territory – to explore the further potential of my life-space? Is this what 'my illness' was for? What do I want to do with the rest of my life? Can I have what I want? I've to go back to St Paul for the answer: 'Not I; but Christ in me.'

I had a strange vivid dream that I would die at 102. Are the intervening years to be fruitful or merely an earthly existence? Who knows? I realize that I must be content to not-know the future but to work today. '"Only be strong and work for I am with you", saith the Lord of Hosts' – what a clarion call to do more creative work! Reassurance came in a dream where I saw a very old apple tree in my childhood garden, covered with ripe red fruit.

One day recently I woke with a stabbing pain in my chest. In my heart? The doctor friend, a cardiologist, to whom I had already spoken about my heart, to see if it was physically affected or not, had asked me in some detail to describe the pain. In reply to his questions I told him it seemed to penetrate 'like the fiery darts of the evil one' stabbing through and through. The analyst in me says, 'Associate stabbing', so here goes. R.L. Stevenson's poem 'The Celestial Surgeon' has been a favourite one with me since I was a girl.

If I have faltered more or less
In my great task of happiness ...

Lord thy most pointed pleasure take
And stab my spirit broad awake.
Or, Lord, if too obdurate I,
Choose thou, before that spirit die,

A piercing pain, a killing sin,
And to my dead heart run them in!

I remember also a quotation from the Old Testament prophet Ezekiel: 'I shall take from you the heart of stone and give you a heart of flesh.' And I have already written about the *stabs* of remorse which seem inevitable in the process of anamnesia, in my case the recovery of memories about my own capacity to love in the early days of my relationships with husband and children. Do we ever love with full caring, centering the awareness on the other rather than ourselves? Is our egocentricity so difficult to shed that 'the other' seldom, if ever, receives full understanding? It is with much difficulty that we can stand in his shoes, find his point of view. How would my life and his life change if we understood all, and forgave all! Let me re-iterate these poignant words. I think again of the phrase 'pangs of remorse.' 'If only' makes no sense. We cannot go back on yesterday, *and we should not try*.

Let us visualize again a scene in Galilee 2000 years ago. A paralysed youth carried by his four friends on a stretcher – a teacher with healing power inside a building so crowded that this party cannot make its way in, but so eager are they that they go to work and lower the stretcher through the roof. What words are spoken? 'Lad, it's all right, you needn't worry about that old story that makes you feel so guilty. Let go of it all.' It dawns on the patient that this is true and when he is told to stand, pack up the stretcher, release his four friends for other business and get on with his own life, amazingly it happens. He walks out a new man: energy, so foolishly used in *pangs of remorse* which result in paralysis, is now set free for his daily tasks.

And birth pangs? Pain and anxiety are inseparable from rebirth and from growth of the psyche. Much has to die so that new life can emerge. 'Never grudge the pangs.' Die so that new life emerges. Something is happening. We are caught – each of us – in the great process of evolution, so that nodal points occur in our conscious ability to choose and decide and take over control from our conditioned, instinctual life-patterns. The crucifixion, the martyrdoms, and the persecutions, the ridicule of new discoveries such as that of Galilio and Copernicus are all nodal points in evolution.

Today you and I may well be standing on a threshold with a new emergent pattern of life. It is with this thought that each of us must approach the task of understanding 'my illness' and gain the courage to accept healing, so setting free energy that may accomplish far more than we can imagine.

8.

What About Dreams?

The Nature of Dreams

What about dreams? Are they important? Can we afford to neglect them? Are we wise to forget our nightmares since they are so disturbing? Do we all dream or only some of us? They don't seem to make sense, so how can we expect to understand them? To both Freud and Jung, the pioneers in exploring the unconscious processes in the psyche, analysis meant dream analysis and I follow in their footsteps. Poor Freud had no analyst till he met Jung, nor had Jung till he met Freud, but between them they have opened up great tracts of unknown country stretching well beyond man's imagination, harbouring and yielding great treasure and riches to our understanding.

With its beginning early in this century across the channel, tentative, uncertain, a network of analysts has established itself. Taking root in our country it greatly strengthened and enlarged its territory with Hitler's action in expelling the Jews. Regretfully we now see that we were not ready to establish the movement and many of the wisest men and women who were open to the new teaching crossed the Atlantic and established this analytic work on the other side. There it gained great recognition, and not only in Washington DC and New York but in the Mid West and in California a great network of analysts exists and grows. Their teaching is flowing back into this country and we have focal centres from which again, slowly perhaps but with great certainty, analytical work is developing. A network of seekers exists and in a quite uncanny way they find others who are aware of their need for psychological knowledge and for those who value their dreams as giving access to the depths of experience. The movement can be symbolized by yeast grains, microscopic and scattered far and wide, with great power to proliferate. The result becomes visible and obvious, sometimes amazing.

Dream analysis opens up people's lives as yeast opens up the dough. People tell me that only once in their lives has a dream been analysed but from that moment their life seemed to take a fresh turning. When we talk of 'well analysed persons' we think of those who have come into the field because of their own need, their own problems and anxieties and through their dream work have found the liberation of creativity, whose energy is available, whose horizons have widened. Such people *are* yeast leavening society, opening the minds and hearts of those they meet into new areas, the dimensions of the Spirit.

Dreams have been recorded since time immemorial. In our Bible we read of Jacob's dream where the angels went up and down the heavenly ladder. Pharaoh's servants dreamed about their own problems but Pharaoh himself had 'big dreams' affecting the nation. Our present commitment to discovering the meaning of dreams dates from the turn of the century when the Viennese physician Sigmund Freud began to listen to his patients' dreams. The listening indicated understanding, and through this, surprisingly but certainly, healing set in and psychotherapy was recognized. Freud demonstrated the value of interpretation by the therapeutic results he obtained.

However, the mechanism of dreaming – what happened in regard to dream activity – was not understood at that time. It was fifty years later that the electro-magnetic activity of the brain was observed and recorded, and the actual happening of the dream observed in terms of brain-waves and eye-movements. So there are two schools of interest in the dream – one focussed on content and the other on mechanism – both dating from the present century, within the life-time of some people who are still living.

We now know that dreaming is a normal function of the psyche. Babies dream almost continuously, while aged folk's dreams may be scanty, but even in their later days very vivid and meaningful. When discussing dreams in ordinary conversation it is common to find people stating that they do not dream or can only remember one or two dreams in a life-time. In the sleep-laboratory, however, the graphic records demonstrate clearly that normal individuals dream on an average four times every night and if wakened when their 'rapid eye movement' (REM) is observed they can remember and recount the subject of their dreaming. It is almost amusing to consider the serious loss of wisdom from the unconscious sleeping area of the psyche lost to us and to mankind in the dark hours of everyday experiences.

What is a dream? In one sense, we still do not know, but there are some things that can be said.

The Dream is the focus of our ego-centricity. It is a gift from the unconscious, in which we see ourselves 'in the round' – good and evil – shining and the shadow – the waiting and the doing – the hunter and the hunted – the finding of the destination and the missing of the train.

Travelling is indeed a very common dream symbolism. Do we travel by air, sea or land? Do we use our own energy – i.e. walking, swimming, bicycling or flying? Or do we rely on energy from outside resources? Wind, petrol, electricity or steam? Is our road uphill or downhill? Are our doors closed? Do they open to us? Have we the key?

How often do we find the unexpected in our dreams? ("I thought it opened into a dark cupboard but instead was a large room that I did not know was there.") Are we afraid of the precipice, or do we discover a path that leads us down? A nightmare discloses something of the cause of our fear. Are our dreams occupied with death – the pregnancy, or birth, the new-born baby, the young child? Or maybe the dying man, the dead body?

I do not propose to go back into the history of dream analysis. Freud and Jung are our masters and their teaching is widely known and accessible through much literature. But here is a story about a man and his dream. I met Joseph at a Sempervivum Easter School five years ago. I had arranged to organize a group of people daily who did not want to be involved in Yoga, which was our chief business that year. Sixteen people gathered for my group, including old friends and patients, but also new additions attending the school for the first time. When we had gathered and made ourselves known to each other I put the question 'What shall we do with this opportunity of an hour and a half given to us for four days? Shall we form a discussion circle or would you like to work with dreams?' A majority voted for dreams, but Joseph looked annoyed, saying that he never dreamed and if he did it was nonsense anyhow. The group soon got interested and I was glad to notice that Jo seemed to pick up the thread and discuss the interpretations. When we parted I suggested that he would dream that night and that he would analyse his dream next morning. Sure enough! He brought a written sheet and the group decided to start the hour with Jo's dream 'I dreamt of a paragon.' 'What?' 'A *paragon*.' 'Oh yes.' 'He was intellectual, musical, artistic, good looking, athletic, well dressed *but* he had an unfortunate habit of driving his car over other people's lawns – yes, and he lived in a glass house.'

The group closed in on him. 'Everyone in the dream is yourself. You are the paragon', they insisted. He seemed not unwilling to accept the role and, if he saw himself in a glass house, he would not mind us having a good look at him as 'paragon.' He had, on the previous day, told us that he was now retired, living in Scotland, but that he had belonged to the U.S.A. Air Force in which he was a bomber-pilot, latterly an instructor. So I said to him 'As a bomber it wasn't any use thinking of the lawns down below?' He took the point, elaborating it and telling us how particularly hard it was to persuade the young trainee pilots to harden their hearts over the damage their bombs were causing – 'to other people's "lawns"'. Having understood his own dream he quickly entered into the spirit of the group. When he said goodbye three days later he asked 'I suppose you know that I am *shattered*?' 'Is it good to be shattered?' I asked. 'Yes, indeed', he replied, 'but what shall I do now?' I directed him to the dream group meeting at the Salisbury Centre in Edinburgh every Wednesday at 5.30 p.m. Next time I attended, Jo was there. He had attached himself to the Centre and was already working in the garden. He has become a fast friend and helps many people in difficulty. He likes me to tell you this story; after all he told us that he lived in a glass house!

Jo's dreams, until shared and interpreted, made no sense. They came from that part of the mind which:

a) we share with others: "the collective unconscious";
b) is irrational;
c) is full of forgotten memories and of unawareness of how our lives function;
d) stores energy, releasing it spasmodically in ways we do not understand or control.

I believe that the dream gives access to this 'unconscious' – the great storehouse of memory, not only personal but racial; the great reservoir of energy, only partly tapped and channelled in everyday life. It is ultimate reality, ultimate wisdom, understanding, love and caring beyond the conception of our ordinary thinking mind. Through experience, wise folk have learned that we do not need to fear the shattering nor the shaking of the foundations. There will be a firmer earthing, a solider foundation.

It is most significant that in the dream death is not final: life returns. We interpret this through the understanding that the psyche, man's spirit, is indestructible. The word *psyche* in Greek originally stood for the cabbage white butterfly! Its life is symbolic of growth, change, transformation: the earth-bound grub on the cabbage leaf, the imprisoned creature, 'liquidated' and re-made in the chrysalis, then the winged creature finding its new potential and its new element, the air.

This psyche in man, that is in you and in me, has its earthiness, its body with all it demands and needs, it has its suffering, its shattering, but when it emerges and comes to itself it discovers its wings, its new dimensions in the world of the spirit. When there is difficulty in recalling dreams it is a good plan to put paper and pencil by the bedside and to give oneself at bedtime the suggestion 'I shall remember and record my dreams.'

All religions postulate that *caring* is inherent in life, love of self, love of others, love that is ultimate reality. Many ages ago Moses taught the Jewish people that love, not fear, was the basis of existence when he said:

'Underneath are the everlasting arms.'

Dream Groups

In 1958 at the Davidson Clinic in Edinburgh a study-circle of ten individuals dealing with P.W. Martin's *Experiment in Depth* developed spontaneously into a Dream Group which carried on for several years. Now in 1980 this has become a dream group movement in Edinburgh and further afield. I am aware of more than a dozen such weekly gatherings. The importance of these groups has been strengthened by the interest shown and the help afforded by Dr Montague Ullman of New York and also by a connection with the Jung-Sanor Dream Group Movement in Berkeley, California.

An important decision has to be made on joining a dream group, since on recounting a dream we take a big risk of exposure; *we give ourselves away* to the other members. Unless we are willing to do this we shall gain nothing by joining – except, maybe, disfavour from our fellow members. Usually I say to a new member 'By giving this dream you have joined the group.'

Extraverted people are unlikely to envisage the possibility, indeed the probability, that the dream they recount will not flatter them but is much more likely to put them to shame. The repressed material with which it deals is usually guilt-laden and therefore is very likely to make them feel bad when it discloses itself. Immediate relief is likely to follow, however, particularly when we say '*Is that all*? Have I been unwilling to face up to a matter, at the time serious, but in the light of present day only a childish misdemeanour or indeed something quite innocent?' Of course this is not by any means always the case and considerable suffering may ensue if dishonesty has been masking the feeling of guilt. An uneasy suspicion in the group that he/she is 'phoney' or hiding the reality gives place to sympathy and a desire to comfort. In this way the group becomes cohesive and strong, supportive in their mutual relationship.

At times there is a tendency to condone the sin or misdeeds, pointing out how common their ill-doing is. It is kinder and wiser while sympathizing to suggest that we 'go into it' and discover the motivation that lay behind the wrong doing. There is great relief in being accepted for what I am, even if it involves shame, rather than for the mask which depicts what I would like others to think of me.

The following story illustrates how one member of a dream

group was helped to solve her problems. Naomi was a widow and blamed herself for lack of love during the ups and downs of married life. When first married they had been intensely and passionately in love and had promised each other that this would last as long as they lived. They had a good married life, but there were periods during the thirty years of marriage when they had seen each other's weaknesses but had settled down into a fairly ordinary comfortable way of life. Before her husband's death, indeed, when separation faced them, there had been a renewal of the passionate early love, and on his death Naomi blamed herself for the drabness of the intervening period, feeling that had she maintained the intensity of caring he need not have died.

Here is Naomi's dream. The setting was in church where a memorial service was being held for a husband. The widow with three other women were sitting in the front pews. They were all dressed in black and she faced the congregation, while the others faced the organ. She was an ugly woman. In the dream the organ, not the preacher, nor the altar, was the focus of attention.

At the end of the service the congregation waited for the outgoing voluntary but there was an awkward pause waiting for something to happen before the music for dismissal began. On leaving the church, Naomi, with her mother, attached themselves to the widow and went part of the way with her, till they came to cross-roads and said goodbye. As they talked the widow expressed indignation with the hospital authorities who had not given her husband adequate treatment which she felt would have saved his life. But Naomi's mother asked 'to let be', as he was now dead, no action could avail. As they parted she continued her journey east while Naomi and her mother faced west, an enormous puddle, a pool of muddy water, confronting them. The mother leapt over it without any trouble but said it would be dangerous for Naomi. Naomi however, went backwards for several yards, then took a running jump and cleared the water landing in her mother's arms and together they went off to their home. The dream depicted very accurately the 'setting' of her childhood life with the church and the different roads.

Here is *the meaning of the dream* as it was worked out in the group. The 'ugly woman' who did not 'face the music' was Naomi herself. She had recently faced the facts of the years of marriage when the early love of married life had given place to an 'ordinary' marital relationship, without intensity of feeling except when separation faced them as it had done in the frequent circumstances which took the husband abroad, and again when death was imminent. The dream depicts her 'fourness' – her integration at the end of her life, but the ugly part of her – she thought of the widow as non-descript and unattractive – was not facing the music (the organ in the dream). Thus it maintained her attitude of paranoia, blaming others for her own guilt about her husband's death.

Naomi, the dreamer, is in the church in the back pew. She, therefore, *is* facing the music, and deeply aware of the inconclusive end of the service until the closing voluntary is played. Identified now with 'the mother' that is with her own maternal function, she sees the necessity to get on with her life, not wasting time and energy in imputing guilt to others. They part at the cross-roads, the widow's face towards the east – the new day.

Mother and daughter, that is, a mature Naomi, go home together, but first 'the puddle' has to be negotiated – which represents no difficulty to the mature woman. Naomi has to go back to find the energy to leap across, like the bowler on the cricket field before he delivers the ball. *'Reculer pour mieux sauter'* is the phrase that describes the analytic process. Naomi had to gain the understanding which would surmount the problem of guilt and set her on the way home – the way to her own true centre which we call 'the self'.

The dream then depicts the dreamer, one aspect of herself, ugly, disapproved, and, as such, facing the group. She is, however, after an awkward delay, brought into touch with the wise mother, and with the dreamer in the here and now of today. So the mourning self is set free to face new life, while Naomi, now wiser through analysis, can find her centricity, her home, from which her life will continue – let us hope with fresh insight because of her dream!

An opening warning at the beginning of this section might well deter you from undertaking the somewhat perilous adventure of joining a dream group, but I trust that Naomi's dream will bring encouragement as you visualize that running jump, landing her safely across the muddy water into her mother's arms and you think about the good advice to take the necessary backward steps in order to get the energy for the next bit of the journey. 'Reculons pour mieux sauter.'

Dreams and Synchronicity
'Co-incidence' means literally a falling together, and 'synchronicity' a coming together in time. They are words that never fail to excite interest. A measure of surprise hits us when, unexpectedly, we meet with two events occurring together to make sense – even, it may be, to solve a problem.

Recently Laurence Becker from the U.S.A., a film director, rang up saying he was in Edinburgh and had been asked by a mutual friend in New Hampshire to get in touch with me when he visited Scotland. I said 'I am having a birthday party today. Come along.' Another guest was Sir George Trevelyan, also 'unexpectedly' in Edinburgh, and these two men had much in common and felt grateful for the meeting. Laurence Becker also talked to me about Laurens van der Post and their mutual deep interest in the Jungian teaching. Three months later, Laurens van der Post was in Edinburgh for the day giving a talk in the evening to launch our project of 'Wellspring'. We had many guests to meet him through the day, but now, sitting quietly with him at tea time, I realized I had not read my morning mail. Opening it, a wad of notes fell out of a U.S.A. airmail envelope along with a letter from Lawrence Becker saying 'These are notes of a lecture that van der Post gave in New York shortly after Jung's death. You may care to have them'. I handed them over to Laurens who said he was delighted to have them as he had searched for them in vain and thought them irretrievably lost!

Then here is a dream co-incidence. In January 1979 just at the beginning of the year I had a 'big dream'. It had to do with the unity of psychology and religion – a matter that interests me greatly. The last image of the dream was of a building, the front of which was a suburban villa, but joined on to it, a church with stained glass windows. A few days later Bishop Neil Russell, who was visiting me, told me how he had recently gone to Craigmillar to celebrate Eucharist. To his surprise the service was not in the church, but in the sitting room of the clergyman's house. After the service the company had lunch together and spent much time talking.

A few days later a young businessman from Australia, spending only a weekend in Edinburgh, told me how his Presbyterian minister in Melbourne had come in contact with methods of psychotherapy and counselling while studying theology in Aberdeen. On his return he was able to appoint thirty young elders to undertake the pastoral congregational duties, while he committed himself to the care of souls through psychotherapy. The old empty church was sold, a new building erected in a populous area, with some rooms set aside for counselling, others for craft and recreational activity, and a large hall for preaching. Within a few weeks after my dream four ministers had visited me eager to talk with me on the subject of psychology and the spiritual life, and an invitation had come asking me to address an international conference on the subject of psychotherapy and religion. It seems obvious that the dream was glimpsing a unity that may well involve me further in this field which awaits exploration, development and fulfilment.

After I had written this, a patient in a dream group, who had not heard my dream, related one in which an ancient castle in Germany and a church of great antiquity were 'all of a piece' under one roof. She told us that she was not a church-goer and thought this referred to the spiritual side of her life, integrated, perhaps, through generations. Nowadays she was seldom in church but she had in no way relinquished her religious heritage and she believed that our dream-group-therapy was now all a part of her 'search for God'.

And here is a family story. I had gone to London for a few days as Dr Graham Howe had asked me to give a talk at 'The Open Way'. 'Come early', he said, 'and meet a few people who will be interested.' He introduced me to someone called Camilla – 'Camilla this is Winifred from Edinburgh. Winifred this is Camilla from Johannesburg' – and he moved away. Conversation proved to be sticky till I said 'What is your surname Camilla?'. 'Oh, one that you have never heard I'm sure – Wybrants.' 'Curiously enough', I replied 'my grandmother had a cousin called Ruby Wybrants whom I remember meeting as a child about 7, but she didn't live in Johannesburg, her home was in Monifeith near Dundee.' Camilla gasped 'That was my father's grandmother. His people came from Monifeith.' Years later Camilla and I are in touch as she has a Group movement in

Jo'burg which is called 'The Open Way'.

Sometimes there seems to be many connecting links. One day Tew Bunnag, who was conducting a Vipassana Meditation workshop, asked me suddenly 'Does the name John Layard mean anything to you?' 'Yes,' I answered. 'John was one of my great friends. He died some years ago. Curiously enough I had been thinking of him today.' 'Well,' said Tew, 'a young friend of mine called Malcolm Ritchie was his secretary, lived with him and cared for him some years before he died, when he was deaf and blind. Malcolm will want to meet you. Yes, of course he will come, though he is living in Cornwall.'

Malcolm and I are now friends and have much in common. He wrote to me recently that he had bought a house in Arran – the very house where my husband and I had spent a holiday about forty years ago and that his next door neighbours were my friends Dan and Irene. Co-incidences.

Why do these things happen? What is the mystery of this co-incidence – the falling together in time or place? It has a feeling of purpose of fulfilment. Quite often it is useful, as when someone 'turns up' with a car when we are stranded, or the telephone rings when we need to get in touch.

We cannot *explain away* these co-incidences but *there is a way of life which allows events to fall into place.* Jung tells us to note them, as they are signposts to reassure us we are on the right road, and Chinese philosophers, similarly, write of them as confirming our sense of direction. When the occurrences *follow* a dream we label the dream precognitive and quote T.S. Elliot:

> Time present and time past
> Are both perhaps present in time future
> And time future contained in time past.

Shall we postulate that co-incidences, like dreams, are a function of the unconscious? The best definition of this area of the psyche is that it is the Unknown. We postulate that it is symbolized by the ocean, in which every drop of water has the potential of meeting any other and merging with it. Like the ocean it is constantly in motion, with waves and currents barely disturbing its unity. Fascinating incidents are recorded of well-corked bottles containing written papers travelling long distances and bringing information from afar. How strange that they should survive unbroken! How unbelievable that the bottle will come into the hands of someone able to read and transmit the message!

Telepathy is, of course, another function of the unconscious. Since the massive statistical accumulation of facts through the work of Professor J.B. Rhine in the U.S.A. it is so acceptable that we cease to marvel at it and say 'only telepathy', taking its operation for granted. Telegrams and telephones have to some extent supplanted telepathy and 'capricious' is an adjective we must apply to all the ways of the unconscious, so that we talk of 'lucky co-incidences', 'fortuitous' or 'a fortunate concatenation of circumstances'. I like to think that Dr Louisa Rhine, wife of Dr J.B. Rhine, who works in this field, collecting instances but not demanding scientific corroboration, had ten files to her husband's one. We cannot limit the dimensions of the unconscious in time, space or other man-made conception – nor pontificate regarding its functions. Man is puny and his mind desperately limited. At the present day the dark area of mind is being intensively explored and light is being directed into strange mysterious corners. The limitations of human potential are expanding with amazing acceleration – frighteningly. Computer science, for instance, was unknown and undeveloped 'yesterday', that is fifty years ago. How quickly we have accepted it as commonplace and how sure we must be of its future use in business technology and, indeed in spheres beyond our imagination, as life unfolds.

I had barely finished writing this when I had a communication from my friend Lawrence Becker in the U.S.A. He wrote these words, he said, after reflecting on some aspects of synchronicity:

If we be true to the integrity of the moment
Who knows what or where
Wonders, beasts, adventures,
Will sweep us up into their flood?

Can we let go of the words that pull us backward – 'If only',

'What if', 'Yes but', and hold instead to the everlasting *Now, He is, Thou art, I am, something is happening!*

9.

Guilt and Forgiveness

One day, a nun in the convent where I was staying stopped me to relate a dream (the nuns all realized my interest in dreams). She told me: 'I was carrying a heavy load up a hill. It weighed me down: I took it and threw it ahead of me so that I was free from it, but again I had to pick it up and throw it ahead till I reached the end of the climb.' We were in the company of others so I did not go into her dream, but she said she thought it had to do with some heavy tasks of the previous day which had taxed her physical strength. I am sure it was a dream about guilt.

Possibly she got rid of her guilt temporarily by confession; but it had always to be taken up again. You may remember that St Paul asks 'How do I rid myself of this burden?' 'Who shall deliver me from this body of death?' St Paul sees the answer in Christ.

Our Lord dealt with guilt as a causation of physical ill-health, equating forgiveness with the ability of the paralytic to find healing. Nowadays we call these illnesses in which we realize the emotions to be causal factors *psychosomatic*. Christ's remedy was forgiveness – 'Thy sins are forgiven thee'. The woman with excessive bleeding over twelve years of her life had to realize that she was not guilty but forgiven: that there was no need for all that loss.

The realization of forgiveness is crucial. It may involve self-forgiveness as well as forgiveness of others, and it is no facile operation. Contrast *'forgive'* with *'forget'*. Is forgetting to be equated with repression, the hiding away of the problem in the 'cellar', Freud's symbol of the personal unconscious? It lies there out of sight, out of mind, but it is not disposed of. Like the nun's burden it has to be dealt with later. Forgiving is different. It involves letting go of our cherished resentments.

Forgive. Only love is strong enough for this giving, as was Christ's love for the healing of the sick. Remember the saying *'Tout comprendre est tout pardonner'.* Our great need for understanding – to understand and to be understood. Isaiah taught us that it is an attribute of the Creator: 'There is no searching of his understanding'.

Might we even guess that God became incarnate in the man Jesus in order that, seeing things from the human standpoint, he could have compassion on mankind? The word *comprendre* – comprehend – involves bringing together and grasps all the human elements that make man sinful.

It is important to note that the prefix 'par' in *pardonner* and 'for' in *'forgive'* indicate 'utterly', while the meaning of 'for' in *forget* is merely negative. So if we equate the meaning of 'forgetting' with repression, it indicates loss: the contents of the cellar are not being used in our lives. The repressed material has become valueless. Are we *listless* because we have repressed and lost our *lust* – our zest for life? Are we restless and disturbed by a gift, an ability, of which we are unaware – music, or some craft for instance – which is longing to be expressed but lies dormant and unused in the unconscious? The frustration which accompanies the repression of our innate abilities is an important factor in much mental suffering, and physical ill-health.

Who are the people whom it is most difficult to forgive? It may be 'those of one's own household', siblings, the children who were born of the same parents. Didn't Freud say 'The crime which no-one can forgive his parents is the crime of having other children?' My own life-experience may serve to illustrate this. I was born third in a family of five with two older brothers and two younger sisters. The brothers teased and provoked me mercilessly. I remember at the age of five asking my mother if this would ever stop. My elder brother was going on a sea-voyage to cure his cough. 'When he comes back will he still be teasing me?' I asked. The grown-ups explained, but they could not *explain away* this suffering. 'They tease you because they love you', I was told. This was my first meeting, perhaps, with the idea of ambivalence–the two-ness of feeling for the same object. The boys were *expected to feel* that their little sister was a darling: *what they did feel* was that she stole parental love and interest which had been focussed on themselves until her unfortunate and unsolicited arrival: 'We ought to love her, but we want to murder her.' When my second brother, at the age of seventy, stated baldly that he had been jealous of me all his life, it came to me–then a full-blown analyst–as almost unbelievable. 'Only a girl', 'Girls are no good', 'Imagine *you* thinking you could do it'. Was all this nothing more or less than the anxiety, the fear that perhaps girls after all *were* highly valued, and might even prove to have more ability than their brothers? Patterns of childhood tend to persist throughout one life, and I recognize this pattern recurring in my relationship with men of all ages, perhaps more noticeably with my near contemporaries. It is as if I *expected* them to look down on me, to belittle my capacity, almost hearing the school-boy language: 'She has good cheek to think she can do it'. These feelings were fortified in the early days of medical training. The practice of medicine was a male prerogative and 'What cheek!' was almost audible as we women medical students entered the class rooms. Women were not accepted in the medical services of the 1914-18 war, but an Edinburgh graduate Dr Elsie Inglis went under the auspices of the Red Cross to the Balkans and served in the Serbian Army and proved that both in the matter of surgical skill and of physical endurance women could stand up to the tests imposed.

Then there were my little sisters. Since my entry into the field of analysis, which began with my own analysis, I have seen that one of my big problems in life has been that of the younger woman threatening to eclipse me by her attainments. I can now in retrospect be aware of my sister catching up with me, stepping on my heels. She was fair, golden-haired and rosy. I was dark and ordinary. She could sing in tune: I had no musical gift. I vaguely remember her entry into the nursery, when I was not yet three. There was a small bath in front of the nursery fire. A white object was being taken out of the water onto a nurse's lap. Perhaps at that moment in my life I had a glimpse of the meaning of *trespass*. Someone had trespassed into my nursery: was it to take a lifetime to forgive her? So throughout my life the younger woman has threatened me, threatened to surpass me, to be more gifted, to acquire greater skill. Sometimes I have loved them dearly, but always there has been the shadow of jealousy. Younger colleagues have threatened to surpass me, and what about my own daughters? I am resistant to the suggestion that I have an ambivalent relationship with them: but I must recognize that there was a trespassing there, too – a moving across the love of husband and wife. The generation to which they belong has had better opportunities than mine; better education, more travelling abroad. They have been in touch, in their youth, with more cultured people of widely different interests. Then of course there are the media through which their knowledge of the world has grown apace. I was first aware of the wireless after I had acquired a family of my own.

Every father knows something of this when he is aware of the love of mother for her child, more especially for the man-child, her son. This boy trespasses – steps in between the early idyllic 'sweetheart' relationship of their wooing and early marriage. Daughters, too, can and all too frequently do, transgress, seducing the husband into being a doting father, causing grief and uneasiness to the mother. When this happens, all three people suffer.

With understanding of what is occurring, parents may wake up to the need for renewal of their love-life and return to earlier 'sweetheart' relationship. If this can be accomplished, the children, too, greatly benefit. They find their right and happy place between the parents and are not in danger of becoming possessed by the parent of the opposite sex. Mother-tied sons, father-tied daughters all too often fail in later life to adjust to their own marriage and parenthood. It is not possible for a son or daughter to maintain, along with the marital situation, a close parental tie which absorbs undue devotion and interest; but it is surely possible to keep respect and love and yet find the way of non-attachment, so then there is freedom to make the new relationship of marriage without being hindered and drawn back into the earlier ties between parent and child.

I can recollect occasions when my own mother would willingly have murdered me in her wrath. It is more difficult to see myself in this relationship to my daughters but I have already said that to forget, that is to repress and banish the feelings into the unconscious, is much easier than to forgive. To understand – I reiterate – to understand is to forgive. Self-understanding is a process that takes all the time granted for living. It is always painful but the pain is more acute in the beginning and eases as we lose our self-importance in old age. It is the pre-requisite of understanding others. We must see ourselves as life's children, trespassing into the lives of the parents. Were we desired, or just another pregnancy? Newborn, we trespassed into the family, which may well have been more peaceful without us; into school as the new boy or girl, upsetting the established order of the class; into our place of work where our colleagues feared we might be more skilful than they or a drag on them; into communities where a new member could upset the balance of power and importance.

So far, we have looked at the negative side of repression, and at the healing which can come when its grip is released. But repression is of course a necessary disciplining and civilizing force in life, balancing the *id* – that is the instinctual forces. The id, libido, life force, psychic energy, derives from the deep powerful cosmic Reality. Just as the grid electricity has to go through transformers before it is wired up in domestic supply so too our spiritual energy needs to meet that which will hold it and make it acceptable, not overwhelming to our lives.

Gentle, wise, understanding parents provide 'holding'. They allow the child to experience his anger but not fear it. He can be aware of its usefulness and need not fear that it murders!

Recently on radio I spoke about this aspect of anger. I said that every time a parent smacked his child the child would *want* to smack him, but nice good children don't hit their parents; that is, they *repress* this instinctive urge to hit back.

James, aged eight, with his grandmother and mother, had listened to the programme. Father was too busy – he was reading in his study. James, when the programme faded out, ran into the other room and started hitting his father. He explained that he had always wanted to hit back and now his father must take it!! Good for James! Good too that his father took the point and didn't retaliate. Something was happening.

Two instances occur to me of this denial of knowledge in early childhood. One concerns a boy and a girl aged seven and five. Their parents were headmaster and matron of a preparatory school and the children had lessons tagging on to the boys' classes. The girl Poppy came to me as a patient in her late teens. I well remember her plaint – 'Mother never had time for us. I only see her skirt disappearing round the nursery door. She was always in a hurry, always involved in the school, literally with no time for us.'

In the leisure of the therapeutic hours, Poppy found time to ask all the questions that her mother had never afforded the leisure to hear and to answer. We spent time re-living Poppy's early curiosity, her need to know. Academics call this the 'epistemological instinct' and say that when it is repressed we cannot learn. Poppy's last dream I remember, though it was dreamed more than thirty years ago. 'I was pushing my way through a dense forest with great difficulty. Suddenly I came out into an open space where the sun was shining. I became aware that a heavy load lay on my shoulders, but, in the sunshine, I had the impulse to dance. So I danced in that open space and the weight fell off my back and I went on my way lightened.' Do you wonder that after thirty years, now an old woman, I am still glad when heavily-burdened folk, weighed down with ignorance and guilt, come to work out their problems with me? The sunny glade in the forest is there for me as well as for them.

The other instance is of ignorance which seemed to extend over a life-time, also in a woman whose questions were not answered in childhood. She was with her younger brother when the father came into the room to tell them that they had a little brother. The girl asked 'Where did he come from?', but the answer was 'It is naughty to ask questions', so she decided against making further enquiries. In spite of long hours of analysis she kept reiterating that she was unable to learn and indeed her capacity to read and to 'take things in' was very limited. The parents in this case felt guilty because this daughter was conceived out of matrimony and in their circle of church-going people this was thought of as sinful. Sex and curiosity are curiously linked in the libido and in her case, probably also in the father's, both instincts were repressed. This patient's capacity for love and marriage did not develop but the story of her life is not entirely sad. She developed a fantasy of a child companion who went with her into the country and with whom she had the great happiness of showing the beauties of nature and of answering questions. My impotence as an analyst over many years had to be acknowledged, but when the patient became again the little child *with her need to know*, then, as always, something happened and happiness instead of despair supervened in her life.

One of the most dramatic instances of the importance and power of forgiveness for a patient in analysis is provided in the story of Anne.

Anne is a retired school teacher, now in her sixties. Throughout life she has been much perplexed by her relationship with her mother and also by recurring spells of mental illness. She made endless efforts to please her mother and improve their relationship but this always seemed to be a losing battle. The mother always made it plain that Anne did not 'measure up'. Anne described her efforts to help her mother as being 'like putting her goods into a bag with holes in it'. In her mother Anne found an inexplicable barrier, though she always saw her as being so friendly and pleasant to all others, except the closest members of the family. Till the mother's death some years ago Anne poured every care and attention on her, though she herself lived her life 'tortured in spirit' from rejection and disapproval which she could not understand.

Recently in the course of analysis she released and relived an amazing happening of childhood when she was nine years of age. She and her mother attended morning church service in the town in the West of Scotland where the family then lived. Following the service a visitor from overseas spoke with Anne's mother. He had been a former suitor with whom the mother was much in love, but she had refused to marry him as he was going abroad. When it came to the point in memory of the mother shaking hands with this man in farewell and saying, 'I will *never* forget you. I would not go with you then, but I would go to the ends of the earth with you now, instead of what I have to live with for the rest of my days', Anne was completely overcome with emotional distress. She wept continuously for nine hours till at last she retired to bed. During the following two days, at intervals during her household tasks, she broke down from time to time weeping, till at last it seemed her distress was over.

She also recalled clearly the memory of her mother talking with her on the way home about how nice this man was and how she wished she had married him. On arrival home the mother told the father about meeting this old friend. Anne was then taken by her father to another room where sitting on a chair with Anne standing before him, he questioned her closely about the events of the morning and the conversation she had heard. At his mercy, she told all, without any ideas of the implications. The father, seized with jealous rage, confronted the mother, denounced her fiercely and struck her. The mother laid the blame at Anne's door and in fact said, 'I'll make you suffer for this.' This promise she implemented.

Anne had imprisoned this disaster in her unconscious and in many ways was imprisoned by it. Reliving this memory has given her a new perspective. But all the tears she shed when it was recalled were of compassion for her mother, regardless of what she herself suffered at her hands. The nebulous area of shortcoming or failure in her life has now gone. She wishes the matter had come to light years ago so that she could have apologized to her mother and helped her towards a forgiving attitude as she herself now forgives her mother and bears no grudge. She quite rightly feels that with appropriate help at an earlier stage the repeated spells of illness would most probably never have happened.

10.

Do You Love Me?

One day, a patient whom I shall call Amanda recalled that at our first interview – five years before, I had talked to her about love. She had thought 'How strange! A psychiatrist talks about love. What is it? Is she talking about sex?'

Amanda had been born and reared without love. Her mother, one of a large family, had been rejected as an infant and sent to a farm at a distance where in course of time she became an unpaid and unloved servant. Without love she married, and her husband became alcoholic – the important factor probably being his wife's frigidity. Amanda's sister was 'clever' and given the best education they could afford. Her younger sibling, a boy, was valued because of his maleness. Amanda in the middle of the family was 'squashed out' as so many middle children tend to be. She had compensated by developing her inherent gifts, including physical beauty and a capacity for clear thinking.

She had married, in her early twenties, a man who equated love with sex, in his case a compulsive activity. Her early deprivation of love from the parents was reinforced by the denial of opportunity to develop through a loving mating relationship. Her capacity for loving was not elicited in the marriage but only later, when the suffering of her son John, a stammerer, arousing her pity and also her guilt, saddened her and brought her for help. John, born prematurely, had been nursed in an incubator, separated from her at birth. Breast feeding had not been established so that the skin-to-skin awakening of love for her child was in abeyance; but it broke through in her suffering for his disability. In the course of analysis she gradually became aware of further stirrings of feeling and of tenderness until a change in the whole family became evident as the ice of an unfeeling relationship gradually but surely melted away. Amanda's story sheds light on the question 'Do you love me?'

Implicitly this may be the child's first question to his parents. Explicitly the parents may use it as blackmail to the child. The lover stakes his all on the answer. Late in life the husband needs terribly to know. 'Yes,' she says, 'haven't I borne your children? Haven't I cooked for you and fed you? Haven't I been faithful to you all these years?' 'Yes,' he still demands, 'But do you love me?' The question is also asked of friends. Friends? Can we trust our friendship? Is it based on self-love, or on dependency, or on convenience? Or where does it really lie?

Another question – perhaps it should have come first – is: 'Do I love myself?' Let us remember that in both Old and New Testaments the behest is: 'Thou shalt love thy neighbour *as thyself*' – yet is there not an echo of disapproval, a rebuke from the superego, when we claim the prerogative of self-love? It may however, be seen as a birthright. A child born into the centre of a loving circle will know himself to be loved, and his satisfaction with what he is receiving will establish in him the awareness, it may be the certainty, that he is lovable. His self-love at this stage is completely desirable and valuable, it centres his life and from that centre he will grow outward and learn to love others. He will meet the world with a sense of equality, ideally without envy or jealousy, since he is assured that he is accepted.

How sadly different is the case of the unwanted, unloved, rejected infant with no warm loving circle to take him in their arms. Sadly unloved, how is he to learn to love himself? It may well be that he will go through life seeking for that recognition yet perhaps unable to accept it. People will call him egocentric, self-seeking. He is seeking for the centering of which he was deprived at birth.

A third question now presents itself. 'What is my *capacity* for love, for giving, for taking, for sharing love?' We must go on to consider how much this capacity depends on the very first experience of our lives. Did our parents conceive us in love? When we were born did they receive us in loving arms?' 'Love lies,' they say, 'in the contact between one skin and another.' Was the mother's breast available? Were her hands gentle and tender in their touch? Was she there when we needed her? Was there a caring father? The capacity or ability to love and be loved is indeed part of the inherited nature, but it needs to be nurtured and developed in contact with the parents in the first days of life. Vulnerable, it is easily damaged in its growth, even in a loving family. The child who is institutionalised, handled by whoever happens to be on duty, lacks the awareness, the touch of the *one*, the mother or mother surrogate, recognizable by the sound of her voice, the touch of her hands and even more immediately the smell of her body. We partially lose this last-named sense as we grow to adulthood but are immensely sensitive to it in early life. The capacity for loving is instinctive but as I have said, in common with other instincts it may lie dormant if not elicited and developed in infancy.

The tragedy of repression may also overtake it in early life. Discouragement or disapproval in an unloving environment may 'quench the smoking flax' and the flame of love, undiscovered and untended, may die out. It is good to remember, however, that psychologically nothing dies: it awaits the opportunity of development and new life. 'It never grows again' is true of an amputated finger but not of the capacity to love. The lizards, closer to life's beginnings in evolution, do regrow their damaged limbs. So let us take heart on behalf of deprived children. Not only Amanda but her mother and her sons shared in the healing brought about by love and understanding.

Am I a loving person? Am I capable of self-giving? These questions stab our hearts and it takes honesty to find an answer. Should the answer be 'No, I have no capacity for love', then another query presents itself. Is a child unloved at birth then condemned to be incapable of making loving relationships throughout life? We have used the word 'Mother-surrogate', which implies that another person takes the place of the woman who has given the child birth, devoting herself– it might even be *him*self – to the demands of the child by day and by night for the first years of his life. To the extent that such devotion is given there is little doubt that the child would respond with love. The younger the infant is at the time of this take-over from his mother the better the hope for this flowering. For adopting parents the timing of adoption is of great importance; the sooner the infant is re-assured of devoted love the more he is able to respond.

Other crucial epochs in life are the entrance into nursery schools or infant classes. The child is aware of the gentleness or harshness of his reception, and sensitive as to how he is welcomed. Any word of disapproval or dislike is likely to wound feeling – and the growth of love.

Falling in love is a major crisis point in life and here again the meeting of man and woman makes both of them vulnerable to the opening up of the love instinct through the awakening of sexuality. Does he care? Does she care? Is there self-giving or only demanding? It may be this is the great opportunity for the birth of love which has been checked and hindered in the earlier days.

The discovery that 'I am unloving,' may be even more painful than the awareness that 'I am not loved.' Here again, as at birth, at this crisis point, closeness of physical contact stimulates and awakens love, but now other dimensions are even more important, contact in the thought processes, in ideas, in enthusiasms, and beyond this again the affinity for love is primarily a function of the spirit. In the teaching of St Paul we learn that love is pre-eminently a fruit of God's spirit. When the Christ lives in our hearts then we are awakened to love in full measure. This is the love that leaves no room for anxiety, but brings with it the other 'harvestings' of the spirit – joy, peace, patience, kindness, goodness, faithfulness, gentleness and self-control. God's love for mankind, for you and for me, is mediated through our parents and through all who love us, and it takes a life-time and longer to come to a full realization that we love because God first loved us – that our power of loving is the response to His love mediated through our human relationship and deeper still through life itself. The last question that the risen Christ put to his disciple was just this 'Do you love me, Peter?' 'Yes? Then feed my lambs – my little ones.' Peter's love was accepted and his task given.

The good life consists in taking, holding and giving again and when the gift is received and accepted with gratitude then the cycle is complete. Christ taught this lesson just before His passion. Perhaps He was saying that we must look for the opportunity to give, recognize that we are always in touch with hungry starving thirsty folk whose need is for the bread of life, the living water. Everywhere we shall meet the naked people in the rags of their own righteousness and self-sufficiency. Can we show them 'the wedding garment' that is the gift of holiness, available if we answer 'Yes' when it is offered through Christ? Daily we meet people who think of themselves as strangers, sensing their inferiority, unable to mix with others. Can we 'take them in', befriend these sick people? Perhaps we too have healing power or can take them to be healed. In prison? We pray, 'Deliver us, set us free, from evil'. Christ is the liberator – we must bring them in touch with Him. When we have given to those in need we shall see, behind them all, the hand of God stretched out to take what we are giving and are reassured that our gifts are received – the cycle complete.

Self-love is needed at the beginning but it is relinquished as neighbour-love develops – and so we come to fulfilment – the taking, holding and giving of God's love through which we enter into His Kingdom, entering as promised into 'The joy of the Lord'.

11.

The Seven Deadly Sins

> There is nothing either good or bad but thinking makes it so.
>
> *Hamlet*

Morality talks about sin, psychology about guilt. Morality judges that actions are evil or good – psychology allows that there are categories of higher and lower. Morality is sure about right and wrong. Psychology hesitates, observing the conditions and questioning the time and place of the action.

What is *sin*? The word is thought to be allied to 'sunder.' An Aberdeen friend tells me that in her part of the world this word is actually pronounced 'sinder.' Sin then is behaviour which separates us from God, or so at least we think, just as the naughty child feels himself separated from his mother, out of favour, expecting punishment.

Psychologically, I think sin may be equated with egocentricity, the immature unwillingness to conform to the law, the false assumption of one's own rightness, the claim to be 'a very special person' instead of the realization that the sharing is what makes for happiness and well-being.

The endless days of human evolution have taken from man much of the sensory perception with which the earlier forms of life were endowed. His vision is less developed than that of the fly or the bird – his acuity of hearing much poorer than that of his friend the dog, or of the wild creatures. Smell, once so important when the creature was four-footed and kept his nose to the ground, no longer dominates the track he must follow. Similarly, touch and taste have lost their poignancy. What has taken their place in man, as we saw earlier in this book, is capacity *to think, to choose, to make decisions, and to be conscious* in a degree denied to the animals. The creatures are conceded some degree of knowing but the philosophers tell us that only man *knows that he knows*. The creatures follow their instinctual patterns handed down through infinitely long genetic inheritance. Man has to some extent lost contact with his instincts, although to be sure he is much more strongly motivated and dominated by them than at times he is willing to admit. His pride tends to force him to alienate himself from Brother Wolf or Brother Bull, yet these come into his dreams to remind him of his forebears. Consider the curious fact that every spider weaves a web of extraordinary delicacy and intricacy but cannot mend it if it is torn. The pattern can be produced and reproduced, but suffers no interference. Only a few men can weave with a similar skill, but they can repair the torn fabric – a gift denied to the spider.

Evolution is no straight steep path upwards; the path dips before it again ascends. The achievement of the insects apparently ends when their patterns of behaviour reach a maximum of usefulness for the community. The bees and the termites have developed marvellous ways of life, we can even call them perfect, but they are now fixed in patterns that do not develop. Man's patterns develop, his instinctual life shows an ability to change for better or worse, to find ways of sublimation on the one hand or of degradation on the other – depending it may be as to whether he is living with a spirit that cares for others, with altruism and love, or with a focus on the things that matter only to himself, his ego-centricity, self-centredness, in which he is isolated and all-important.

The medieval church in its efforts towards establishing morality listed the Seven Deadly Sins – presumably in an effort to deter people from wrong by fear of destruction. They were pride, envy, anger, sloth, avarice, gluttony and lechery. Nowadays we are more likely to talk of them as symptoms of neurosis and inferiority. There may still be a tendency to blame people for these failings, but their 'sins', if some insight and resource is available, lead the sufferers to the psychotherapist in a demand for help, rather than to a priest for absolution. Let us look then at the Seven Deadly Sins in this light.

Pride we discover is an over-compensation for inferiority, an effort not only to be on equal terms with our neighbour, but to be superior, to be able to look down on him from an imagined height, 'uppish.' The Chinese are said to have a proverb 'Don't stand on a pedestal. One step may be fatal' – and we say 'Pride comes before a fall'. It will be a marvellous day when, rid of both inferiority and its over-compensating superiority, we can find 'the mean of common humanity', walking with our fellows on the high road of life, experiencing the blessed state of equality.

Anger comes under quite a different category from pride. It is an element in human nature that responds to frustration. Not only humans but animals can be very angry. It is of great value in frightening our enemies and in enabling us to mobilize our own resources for battle. Serving a purpose it is an acceptable element, it can be disciplined and used without violence or destructive ill-will. Paul's exhortation to the early Christians 'Be angry and sin not' has fresh light cast upon it by this understanding of the value of anger.

The angry child however is not *persona grata* in the house or nursery, tantrums are frowned upon and possibly punished. The disallowed anger is repressed and no longer available. Like fire, anger is a good servant but a bad master.

As we have seen in Chapter 5, Freud said that what was repressed was relegated to the 'cellar.' Deep freezing was unknown in the Vienna of his day, or perhaps he might have used it as an even more apposite symbol! The material which is put into deep freeze in past years emerges again today as fresh and unchanged as when it was put away, unaffected by the passage of time. Likewise, repressed childish anger escapes the maturing influences of the life-time.

Let us suppose then that a child of three or four (an angry age in life) is smacked and told 'You can't behave like that' and decides that in order to be in favour with the grown-ups he won't behave like that, will not allow his anger to show itself, rejects the feeling, disallows its validity. He and his parents may *forget* (that is *deny*) that he was/is an angry child. If, on the contrary, they hold him gently in his anger, allowing it to be experienced when occasion demands, it will gradually lose its demonic force, it will mature, and losing his fear of its power the growing child will use it creatively, and usefully in adult life. Anger can be gentle when used consciously in the mature human being.

Something more, however, is happening. As the early causes of anxiety are discovered and dealt with, even quite early in analytic treatment it is noticeable, as I have already said, that the patient becomes more actively creative. The longing to do things and to make things asserts itself. Scots folk call a poet a 'makar' and quite often the poet, long since forgotten, asserts himself and makes poetry, the 'inartistic' individual paints, fresh interest develops in many aspects of life. Listlessness disappears and the more lusty individual emerges as the repressions lift. It must be remembered that things don't just *fall* into the unconscious; they are put there and held down there. Effort is involved when a guilty feeling is repressed, effort to push it out of mind, that is to banish it from consciousness, and also continuing effort to keep it from re-appearing. So the available energy, so valuable in tackling the day's work, is used instead in the repression, the forced forgetfulness, and also in keeping the feeling down, resisting its re-appearance, so as to maintain our equanimity.

What a lot of energy we must be wasting in this process! But we have seen that in the work of analysis *anamnesia* occurs, the breaking up of forgetfulness, the release of repressed material so that energy is now available, the energy that has been holding down the memory as well as the energy attached originally to the object pushed so ruthlessly into the unconscious.

Now the libido can flow again, the creative energy so long locked up. Dreams of escape from prison may occur or of keys being found or of 'beneficent rivers of rain.' No longer feared, anger will become his tool, his instrument, his servant and do much to strengthen the fibre of his manhood. I have dealt with this in more detail in Chapter 12.

Sloth, slowness or apathy, is so irritating a quality to overactive impatient parents and teachers that it is easy to see how it comes to be thought of as sinful, or at any rate disapproved and unacceptable. Psychologically we are retarded, and slowed down in thought, speech and action, when we are held in indecision or conflict. We hesitate, not knowing which way to take. It is as if the path before us bifurcates or splits, and we stand there unable to decide whether to go to the right or to the left, frightened to take any risk. In states of depression this symptom is very prominent. It too, has a positive value, since it is a good thing to be able to take time, to wait patiently when no obvious way opens at crisis points in our lives. 'Slow down' can be good advice, slow down at the cross-roads, slow down when intuition warns you of danger ahead: 'Slow down – children crossing'. In our dealings with children it is indeed unwise and often unkind to be in a hurry.

But here again, the waiting may indicate a blockage, a repression. No longer using it wisely and creatively in our lives we find ourselves at its mercy and cannot make the necessary choices or decisions, we are immobilized at the cross-roads not knowing which way to take, seized in a dilemma of uselessness, acceptable neither to ourselves nor to the society in which we live. Where are we to look for deliverance from this grievous situation? As I write this book with its plea for self-knowledge I am trying to find the answer for those who find themselves thus isolated and in the grips of paralytic inaction. 'Know thyself', seek for consciousness. The crossroads are indeed puzzling but, it may be, whichever road we decide to take it will lead us to the Source and to a renewal of life – promised us implicitly in the life-cycle of death and rebirth. 'If winter comes, can Spring be far behind?'

Avarice, or greed, or miserliness, is, like anger, a quality that derives from the instinctual endowment of human nature – the nature which we share with the animals. Notably we remember the squirrels and the jackdaws. The acquisitive instinct, neither good nor bad in itself, may become compulsive and master our lives instead of serving its needs. Healthy, active children pick up shells by the seaside and gather flowers by the wayside if their environment permits. But what about the town children? There is so little for them to pick up and all too frequently it is *naughty* to acquire. 'Don't touch,' 'Keep your fingers off that', are the summons to repression, so that the fingers lose their urge to gather and hold, and a further quota of energy is locked away in the deep freeze.

The positive value of this instinct is seen in the collectors urge to acquire objects – anything from postage stamps to outdated railway engines may be the objects of what he wants to pick up and store. 'This is my latest acquisition' is often on the collector's lips. Similarly, as with anger, the compulsion which we call avarice derives from the return of the repressed instinct escaping from its imprisonment in the unconscious – undisciplined and immature – since it has not been exposed to the rough and tumble of life as it develops.

Gluttony or greed for food has a similar life history. 'I am hungry', 'I need food' are expressions of the primary instinct for life's maintenance. Deprivation may occur early in life, from actual scarcity through famine or poverty, but also because of parental improvidence and lack of empathy, or by digestive disturbances in the child. For one reason or another the child *loses his appetite*, the need and desire to eat is repressed with consequent starvation at some level and, just as in anger and avarice, when the repression slackens and gives way, then the desire returns at an infantile level without the control which comes gradually in the growing-up process. A significant feature in the greedy individual is that he eats without considering the needs of others. The words 'I want', so appropriate in his infancy, still dominate. He has not rid himself of the deprivation and inferiority of his early life and is still unaware of the equal needs and the equal opportunities of his fellows. An experienced psychoanalyst friend of mine used to say 'I am taking the largest piece of cake today – you see I understand my need.' When the psyche is healthy it claims its share in the good things of the world, neither diffident in accepting nor compulsive in seizing, but gladly sharing what life offers.

Envy is the only sin on our list which overlaps the sins which are indicated in the Ten Commandments. 'Thou shalt not covet' warns us against envy. Perhaps it is a sin because it implies that we have no access to the source of all things. The teachings of the Bible encourage us to draw quite directly on this source, 'All things are yours', and psychological wisdom talks of the great resources of the unconscious and its unlimited potential. Envy in its early manifestations is seen when the young child feels resentful because the parents have a relationship he cannot fully share, experiences which they enjoy and from which he is excluded. Sometimes a child's unwillingness to sleep is due to just this, the need to be 'in on it', with what happens after his bed time, and much illness is due to his need to be the centre of parental attention. Obviously this envy extends to the older brothers and sisters who have privileges he does not share, with the wail so common in the nursery years 'It's not fair'.

Children envy not only things they cannot have and experiences denied to them, but also knowledge, the secrets about life which the grown-ups seem unwilling – it may be unable – to impart. When questions are unanswered but refuted with rebuffs such as 'You will know when you are old enough' we can be sure that envy stirs in the child's heart. It is sometimes openly stated that 'It is naughty to ask these questions', more often perhaps parental embarrassment arouses guilt in the questioner, and he is afraid he has 'done something awful' and decides to ask no more questions.

More sharing between rich and poor, between the 'haves' and the 'have nots', between parents and children would help the situation so that there could be less envy in the world.

Envy of course being derived from the instinctual 'I want' of psychic energy has a positive value in life. Gradually the awareness dawns that we too are adult, and no longer under the ban of grown-up superiority. 'All things are yours'. Can we avail ourselves of this wealth through self-knowledge? 'I can do all things through Christ which strengtheneth me' – what a blessed realization that can be. Losing the ego-centricity, the self-centredness of childhood, we can ally ourselves with the energy of the source in the deep unconscious, and find indeed our 'can do' replacing 'I can't'.

Lechery The dictionaries define lechery as 'uncontrolled lust' and I suppose in modern usage we might say 'compulsive sexuality' or 'uninhibited sex', with a slant of disapproval on the whole idea of sexuality. 'Lust' is used here in a similar connotation as 'a bad thing.' When we think about it, it's clear that without sex all higher forms of life would soon die out, and that it, too, comes into the category of an element in our inherited instinctual life, neither good nor bad in itself, quite invaluable when it serves life, but destructive when, becoming compulsive, it dominates our lives. A useful analogy indeed is to be found in the relationship between dog and master. We all dream about animals as symbolic of our animal nature; and the dog seems frequently to signify sexuality although it may, of course, symbolize other qualities such as faithfulness, friendship, or companionship. Let us remember what Edward Carpenter had to say about dog and master, and take to heart his words 'The dog must follow the master, not the master the dog.'

This opens up an area in the psycho-religious field relating to human will – so valuable when controlled and used creatively, but so destructive in the self-willed immature person, still caught in his childish ego-centricity and unaware of his unity with his fellows and with 'that' – the Source in whose will is our peace. 'Lust' is an ambiguous word, disapproved in the definition of lechery as 'uncontrolled lust', but highly approved when we talk of 'a lusty child' and think of Robin Hood as 'a lusty fellow'. When psychic energy is available, flowing in our lives, giving them strength and vitality, then we are lusty. Our poor neurotic friends are listless, that is lacking lust, they say they couldn't care less, the attitude of their bodies gives them away, they look so derelict. They are suffering from the repression of their lust, and with it the loss of the joy of life, the *joie de vivre* which keeps us dancing, and assures us of our part in life's creative purpose.

A great deal of Freud's teaching, as first given to the world, dealt with lust, that is pleasure, and 'unlust', the denial of pleasure. We have to acknowledge a great debt of gratitude to Freud, not least in his work of rescuing sexuality even in its immaturity in the earliest manifestations in childhood. Making us aware of the 'lust' and virility of sexuality and the importance of its presence in adult life, he has done much to rescue it from the shamefulness and disapproval which had accrued to it through the later ages of civilization. Analytical psychology in the hands of Jung greatly broadened the concept of psychic energy but tended to deny the importance of the sexual urge. Later explorers of the unconscious motivation of life varied between the belief that the libido, the flow of psychic energy, is primarily sexual and physical, and the idea that sex is only a tributary to the main energy-giving life stream.

As an example of the disparity let me take *the horse* in dream symbology. This occurs constantly in the work of dream analysis; in Freudian terms it is likely to be interpreted as male sexuality, or as the sexuality of the parent of the sex opposite to the dreamer. In the Freudian analytic interpretation, riding is associated with genital sexual activity, and in a 'fully genitalized subject' the rider and his horse would be perfectly at one.

I well remember how I got into trouble with a Jungian colleague over this interpretation. She was deeply shocked and induced a certain shame in myself as an inexperienced worker. It was implied that I had a very dirty mind! Poor Freud had a lot of this to bear in Vienna when he first promulgated his ideas about infantile sexual fantasies. To the Jungians the horse symbolizes psychic energy in general, and is one of the ways in which we visualize the dynamic activity of life. 'Horse power' is still commonly used as the unit of energy.

How, we must ask, are we to regain the lust, the vitality without which we are so limited in our potential? At certain times and in some parts of the world, the answer seems to be 'through psychoanalysis'. Probably the more constructive work of the analytic movement which began at the beginning of this century lies in the influencing of parents and educators towards becoming more aware of the dangers of repression than in the treatment of repressed individuals. It seems unlikely that there will ever be sufficient numbers of analysts to tackle the immense problems of anxiety, neurosis and psychosomatic illness affecting so great a proportion of the world's population. I agree that analysis is a terribly expensive process in time as well as money. The best answer today may well be to have psychotherapy with a well-trained practitioner. The question of shorter methods which may give reliable results has exercised the minds of all who are aware of the extent of the problem. Recently the method of Human Social Functioning introduced by Eugene Heimler in London and in Calgary, Alberta, has been proving of very great value and spreading rapidly from centres in Great Britain, Canada and Germany.

Dream groups, Transactional analysis, Gestalt therapy, Bioenergetics, Encounter, Primal Therapy, Intensive Journal and apparently endless developments of method to increase man's consciousness are today being used very widely and with great therapeutic value in many parts of the world. These movements are contagious and will increase through their own dynamism. All of them have their origin in our growing awareness of the unconscious motivation of human life, and all owe their dynamics to the activity of the unconscious psychic energy which we call libido, the resource, (or write it 'Resource') which underlies all living processes. Long before Freud, methods were available and were used by men searching for wisdom and increase of spiritual gifts, more particularly in Eastern lands. We call these men mystics, and acknowledge their presence with us through the centuries. Their approach to the unconscious was through meditation, taught in many different schools but essentially alike. Fundamentally meditation imposes stillness, an attitude of waiting and expectancy, and an awareness of the breathing process. All of us can begin to meditate and as we persevere we find the ability increasing. The assurance comes that 'When the disciple is ready he finds his teacher.'

Is our heading still lechery? What had meditation to do with this 'deadly sin'? The answer is that control comes through awareness, that what is conscious can be controlled. Meditation is perhaps the oldest of all methods available for increasing consciousness, it is there for us today together with all the modern ways that are opening and for which we are thankful.

Deadly Sins? Inherent in our psychological awareness is consciousness that the opposites must be contained. *Neurotic symptoms?* We must know the gad-fly which stimulates us to seek for healing and release from anxiety. To talk of the positive aspect of neurosis is not strange today but we can have no desire to remain in the misery of neurotic anxiety any more than it is acceptable to go through life with the devastating burden of guilt on our shoulders, expecting inevitable punishment. Again and again we find ouselves at the crossroads, looking for the signpost wondering whether we can make the right choice. An old Hebrew prophet told his people long ago – 'You will hear a voice behind you saying 'When you turn to the right hand or to the left this is the way – walk ye in it.' Another has said 'A way shall be there and a high way – the wayfaring man though a fool shall not err therein.' And today, as always, the voice of the One who never forsakes mankind is saying 'I am the way'. Crossroads – Is it possible that all lead from centre to circumference, and from circumference to centre?

12.

Aspects of Aggression

In the course of this book I have referred frequently to aggression and anger, and I want now to look in more detail at these elements in our nature.

Death Wishes

Does every anxiety cover a forgotten wish? I can see a small boy, angry at the enforcement of time for bed, screaming as his father carries him upstairs 'I wish you were dead, Daddy, I wish you were dead.'

I can see a small girl threatened by her father's displeasure at her disobedience on his return from business, muttering to herself 'I hope he dies in the train.' Later in life the boy, now adult, worries incessantly about his father's health. The girl, now in her forties, sits by the telephone between 5 and 6pm daily expecting the station master to demand her presence to deal with the corpse. Quite ridiculous, but quite true.

Perhaps you vaguely remember that there were times when you would say 'I wish I were dead'. Today, I wonder, are you afraid of dying?

Many an oppressed and battered wife, many a husband

subject to a tyrannical wife has moaned 'I wish he/she were dead.' When the death occurs there is a great sense of guilt and excessive mourning.

The child does not realize the full import of death. The wish is only that the frustrating punishing parent should be removed, when life would be more comfortable. We ourselves, as adults, frequently dispose of irritating troublesome friends or enemies in this way. 'I could murder that chap' or 'I wish I could attend that woman's funeral'.

Another actual case comes to mind. Jennifer, a woman in her thirties, came to me by train from the country for an hour's treatment twice weekly. Instead of enjoying an hour or two in the town she always came straight to my consulting room from the station and caught the first possible train to return home. When we discussed the necessity of this she referred to her mother's health – a weak heart, she said, and who could tell when it might lead to sudden death? After some months of treatment she had a sudden memory and recalled an incident of her early childhood when she was not yet five. Staying on holiday by the sea were Jennifer, her parents and a woman friend. Father was out sailing when a sudden squall upturned the boat. He was rescued, but his woman companion was drowned. Jennifer thought it was her mother. She was able to recall quite a brief spell in which she was glad about this: '*Now* I can really be 'Daddy's wee wifie'' (a term of endearment he used), 'I can pour out the tea. I can sleep in his bed at night.' Recalling the incident thirty years later she is sure it was one of intense pleasure. But mother was quite safe, she had only been out shopping when the other woman had been drowned. So strong was the mother's heart that she survived for another thirty or more years. The daughter was released from her anxiety and able to take on work which necessitates long absences from home.

Recently a child of three coming into my house greeted me with the statement 'I don't like you', and as she met other people this formula was repeated 'I don't like you'. Children do not like other people interfering in the relationship between the parent and themselves. Conventional mothers insist that their children make polite remarks and give polite greetings, and they teach them that to be 'nice children', acceptable socially, they must repress their bad feelings and substitute polite behaviour. By watching our dreams, particularly these in which we figure as young children and allowing memories, at first indistinct, to take on clarity and importance it is possible to get glimpses of ourselves in the life of our infancy. We shall come to grieve for the wounds that were inflicted upon us, but we shall also come to know ourselves, in some better days, light hearts and gay, aware of the sunshine and sweet smelling bright flowers, remembering kind looks, kind words, sweet singing, gentle efforts at understanding.

In so remembering the light and the darkness of the early days we establish ourselves more securely in life and learn, perhaps, to laugh – sometimes at least – at the grown-up pessimist all too frequently only half-alive, half-awake to the awareness that life can be great fun? Again we must say *'reculer pour mieux sauter'*: we must go back and find our feet, find a firmer stance from which our lives can find new opportunities, new beginnings. We must put ourselves once again into the shoes of the little child and hope to find our way into 'the kingdom' – that mysterious life in which love has somehow won its victory, and the seed – even as small as the mustard seed – has thrust its roots into the earth and grown into a great fruit-bearing tree.

The wish forgotten, repressed, lost in the deep unconscious, has uncanny disturbing power, giving rise to foolish unnecessary anxieties. When it is remembered, it can be recognised as unbelievably childish and ridiculous and relinquishes its capacity to distress us as adults.

Love and Hate

Murder is all the news just now – to open a daily paper and not find at least one murder is the exception rather than the rule. The age of the murderers seem to get less and less. Small boys murder their baby brothers and sisters in the cot, or 'by accident' push them to death in the pram. At all ages of childhood some such violent disaster may occur and when the teenagers come on the scene their murderous activities become astonishing and horrifying. Even more distressing and upsetting to our ideas of civilized life are the stories of the battered babies. In one such case, a dead child was found to have several broken bones and multiple bruises which had been inflicted by her mother living unhappily with her so-called lover. We, representing society, get worked up about these terrible events and are quite sure something must be done to prevent them or at any rate to stop their increase. What is to be done and where we start are not plainly seen nor agreed on.

Capital punishment has been abolished but we are uneasy about that, and many agitate for its re-introduction. Life sentences in prison with deprivation of liberty and hard labour are imposed but we wonder if that is punishment enough for the crime. We cannot make it too hard for these people; we say their crime demands deprivation and suffering. Idealists plead for some other answer to the problem and ask whether it is not possible to find a way of redemption, that is bringing back these derelicts into useful creative human life. On some people's tongues 'You are an idealist' seems to imply 'You are an idiot'. In the Sermon on the Mount there is an attempt to categorize the degrees of guilt or blame-worthiness and also the suitable judgements in each case. *First* the murderers – those who kill their brothers and the ruling is that they should be confronted by their fellows in the local court. *Second* the superior arrogant folk who shout 'Nit-wit' at their brothers, perhaps the idealists are included in the nit-wits. For such it is ruled that they should be taken to the High Court – in the Biblical days this was the Sanhedrin in Jerusalem. *Thirdly* those who label their brothers *atheists* because their conception of God has changed and they are no longer orthodox in their beliefs or theology; for them hellfire.

From this we can assume that there are worse things in life than murder. One of them may be arrogant superiority – projecting onto others our own inferiority which we find it impossible to face. Such an attitude is blameworthy and likely to be condemned by 'the High Courts', that is by people with insight and awareness of the innate equality of mankind. All of us are endowed, in our instinctual life, with the fundamental urges and emotions of love and of hate, the caringness of the parent, the mutual attraction of male and female in sex, our curiosity, our acquisitiveness and combativeness.

Why do we label other people atheist, irreligious, heathen? Why do we judge them and deny them God's acceptance? Is it because we have lost sight of true religion, the way of love and faith and hope, substituting law for love, and morality for the need to understand our fellow men? It is hell to lose the sense of equality with others, maintaining the self-centredness of the immature, and hell to be unaware of the presence of 'That', infinitely more than ourselves, which we call God.

Brother is the operative word in the passage to which I referred above: hating the brother, despising the brother and giving him the status of outcast. The fatherhood of God implies the brotherhood of man. All men are brothers and brotherly love is conceived as a norm in family life. One of the first stories in The Bible is however the story of brotherly hate – Cain and Abel. Yet hate and love, love and hate are strangely connected in human nature. Unless a man can hate how can he love? Frequently, we attach both emotions to the same person – puzzling to ourselves as well as to the onlooker. This 'two-ness' – we call it 'ambivalence' – resembles the heads and tails of the penny. Heads uppermost, we cannot see the tails, and with tails uppermost then head is lost. All of us have some awareness of this in our own emotional experience whether as parents, children or lovers. Loving him today can we face the fact that we hated him yesterday? Hating him now and wishing he were dead can we recollect how dear he seemed to us in a so recent past?

The new baby as he trespasses into the family brings with him this problem for his siblings. They are encouraged to see him as an object of love, even of adoration and so indeed he is. Another side of the coin sooner or later presents itself when it becomes clear that *he* is the centre of the family picture and that *I* have lost that enviable position. It is very naughty to hit your little brother and hurt him when no one is looking; and you may be punished for this behaviour – all very uncomfortable and perplexing, the more so because you know he really *is* someone you care for and want to befriend.

Parents as well as children are caught up in this ambivalence. One bit of them rejoices in their parenthood and truly loves the child, but how irritating he can be, and how frustrating it is to give up your own desires in order to satisfy his needs! All too certainly he invades the territory once sacred to husband and wife and each child as he comes into the family is a trespasser who needs to be forgiven for his intrusion. In the Sermon on the Mount the punishment for murder is less severe than that for being superior and looking down on your brother, less harsh too than for those who are 'unco guid' like the Pharisee who thanks God he is not as other men. Are all human beings perhaps potential murderers, since all are endowed with hate and anger? Expressing it openly we kill others; repressing it, we develop self-hatred and become impotent – killing off our own life energy. So the answer may be to acknowledge this inborn instinct – basic but not base – allowing ourselves to acknowledge it to ourselves day by day. As we become conscious of it we gain control and use it creatively since common with all other instincts anger is a good servant, a bad master.

I remember very clearly that as I carried a young son – less than a year old – he did something which I forget but of which I disapproved. I smacked his hand lightly enough, I think, but just indicating that it was disapproved behaviour. Quick as thought he smacked me in return and I experienced a moment of insight. 'When you smack him he will want to smack you. Nice well-behaved children are taught that this is *not* the done thing – not acceptable in society. But you cannot eradicate his *feeling*: he *wants* to smack you back.' The parents of adolescents enduring the onslaught of their aggression may need to realize that their erstwhile infant is now in his teens getting his own back, which is painful but perhaps inevitable. Adolescence is often talked of as the age of delinquency but let us remember it is also a time of opportunity, a time when perhaps we can hesitate before we punish and realize again that his resentment can only be increased when we hit out at him physically or otherwise. We humiliate him terribly when instead of treating him as equal and respecting whatever maturity he has attained we again punish. In my consulting room I have listened to adult men still shouting with rage that they hate their fathers and could murder them. Why? These scenes occur in analysis when buried memories return with the repressed emotion and the terrible feelings of humiliation, frustration, the denial of their manhood come to consciousness. I remember one such man telling me with relish that he had put three tons of granite on his father's grave! Our repressions are like that granite, bad murderous anger can break through and murder is done. How *can* we treat the murderer? Punishment, life imprisonment, denial of their manhood, humiliation, again breed hate. Granite-walled prisons, uniformed officers, powerful governors, tremendous forces employed in imprisoning our fellow men, keeping them out of the main stream of human activity *Cui bono?* For no one's good, only loss. What can we do? Will no one answer that question?

Many attempts are undoubtedly being made to solve the problem meeting, sadly, with little or no success. Must we then *go back* to the mother, father, child situation? All building-construction depends on the science of trigonometry. The original trigone, the triangle, is the family. Can we, any one of us who understand, devote some at least of our life-energy to working in this field, helping parents to understand and be responsible for the children to whom they have given life? *Reculer* – go back and remember how you felt when punished or separated from your parents. You 'recoil' from such memories, but only by facing them and being willing for the new ways of love and understanding can society, mankind be redeemed. Is it a hopeless situation? Not entirely. Remember that 'God will forgive us all but our despair' and do all you can today, here and now, to tackle at least one triangle that has lost its shape and cannot be used in the building.

There is great need for support to parents, play centres, nursery schools, baby sitters, kind neighbours who will welcome children into their homes. There is also great need for better housing (how infinitely sad that some families have no home). High rise accommodation is a desperate expedient for families – involving great restriction of freedom and making play under the open sky almost impossible. Awareness of how things really are may be terribly disturbing but we have no right to shut ourselves off from it, and, *if we care enough* then disturbance will provoke action and *something will happen.*

The question again must be faced: who are the murderers? Let us face the possibility of projection – that is, shuffling the blame on to others. Once driving my car in bright sunlight I saw approaching me a car with its headlights blazing. 'What fools people are'. As I muttered this to myself; I suddenly realized that it was the reflection of my own car in a big shop window. Oh dear! Can it be me? The more furiously angry we are with others the more likely it is that we are projecting, seeing our own follies and faults in them. Next time we are indignant, *really* hot under the collar, about our neighbours' misdoings we had better just stop and ask again 'Can it be me?' Each time this happens we become just a little bit more aware of ourselves as we really are, thereby gaining strength and vitality.

Whatever our creed or religion, whatever our orientation in the process of life, just because we are human beings we know that peace is better than war, that love is better than hate, creativity rather than destruction. Life is given us, it may be, to see the victory of love over hate and to understand better what Christ means when He says 'I am with you always' that human beings have access to a strength, a power not their own. Christians call it 'Christ in us'. Psychologists mutter about the archetypes in the collective unconscious, and when we practice its presence we discover its reality.

Constructive Aggression

In conversation with individuals, in analytic groups and in the situation of personal analysis, I find myself insisting that we look at the root meaning of *ag-gression* – the Latin *ad* – towards, *gradus* – a step. The word then signifies relationship, an I-thou situation without a necessary connotation of violence or destruction. Like all our instinctual drives, the content of the libido, of our psychic energy aggression is neither good nor bad in itself. It can be used creatively or destructively. Without it we are spineless, flaccid creatures. It endows us with resilience and strength.

Aggression is like fire – *a good servant* – as when it boils our pot and cooks our food; but a *bad master* when it burns up our house and our possessions, or the forests, with such devastation.

One of my own dreams is relevant. In a dream group the young men had been describing the joys of underwater swimming and I had told them that Cousteau's first book came into my hands when it was published and that I regretted my only adventures of this sort had been in the deep sea of the unconscious, which I had been exploring now for many years. So that night I dreamed that I was young again, naked, unclothed, swimming freely, happily, gracefully in deep waters – it seemed to be in the Channel off the Cornish coast as it breaks through into the Atlantic ocean. In the dream I became aware of a shoal of sardines, very pale-coloured small fish. I thought of them as boneless, spineless creatures. Coming to meet them was a shoal of larger fish, possibly mackerel or haddock. The word 'battle' was in my mind and the idea of a hopeless encounter. However, another shoal came on the scene, fish about the same size as the sardines but bullet-nosed, dark coloured, ugly with a front of warty armour. They were called 'benedictines'. 'Allies' was the next word, they were allying themselves with the sardines. That was enough, the big fish turned tail and swam away – no battle, no destruction. The word 'benedictine' I interpreted (still dreaming) as 'softly spoken'. Anger – aggression – need not be violent; it is a useful ally to the spineless who otherwise would fare badly if they joined battle with their overwhelmingly large enemies. The sardines did not need to fight, nor did the benedictines. An alliance was necessary – a consciousness of their resources. The battle was won without fighting.

I can tell you a similar story from real life. Matilda was a child who was always good. In her angry days at the age of three she had been well smacked if she showed any sign of tantrums or bad temper. To be good and well behaved was essential for the approval of the parents. She developed little initiative and married, while still very young, a man whose ideal was to be master in his own house. She colluded in this and became completely passive and accepted his domination, even condoning his unfaithfulness and accepting the idea that she was his property. He bought her over-expensive make-up and clothes that he considered made her look a distinguished wife – but gave her nothing she really wanted and treated her more like a slave than an equal. The children of course suffered as is inevitable in such a marriage and it was because of their difficulties that she presented herself asking for help. Her own difficulties were deep-seated and the process of analysis laid bare great suffering, not only in her own childhood but in that of both parents. The analysis also disclosed great potential in Matilda which in early life had not been allowed to mature and develop but was now making itself evident as her maternal care for her children came to life. Her many talents became obvious and she was capable of great insight into the difficulties of her own and other people's lives. Ultimately the *aggression* woke up and came to her aid. Like the 'benedictines' of my dream it was usually softly spoken. *She* thought of it as ugly and wicked. At times she was shocked at the way she stood up to her husband's cruelty and lack of good feeling. The strange thing is that as her aggression became evident, he became – slowly it is true – less violent, less demanding, even at times apologetic about his behaviour. It was no longer a door-mat marriage, she no longer *colluded* with his denial of her rights. The children's problems began to right themselves so that they became valued members of their school community and the family set fair for better days.

Aggression has its ugly side but when it is *allied* to our spinelessness many of our enemies turn tail – another battle does not need to be fought.

13.

Being Content to Not-know

When I began to write this chapter, barely a month had passed since the election and installation of a new Pope on the throne of St Peter in Rome. Who would have thought that, within weeks, his body would lie dead in the Vatican while the cardinals turned again to Rome to elect another pontiff? We live constantly in this condition of not-knowing what is about to happen. Our whole world may change overnight, the old landmarks may be destroyed and we do not know on what path we shall now travel. We do not even know whether life or death lies before us at this moment. Even the 'here and now' of this moment is transitory. Only one thing about the future seems to be certain – *its uncertainty*.

Sometimes we talk glibly about the unconscious. Let us realize that it is the great unknown (but not entirely unknowable) aspect of existence which extends, not only in the dimensions of human life, but far beyond into dimensions which the human mind seems unable to reach or assess. It lies around us in our infancy. Consciousness only breaks in on us slowly through the impingement of the outer world, but beyond it lies a territory infinitely unknown to us today. As I have already indicated in Map of the Psyche, individual life is given us to explore the world of outer reality and to carry into it the wealth of the inner world. The infant, aware of his mother only, slowly and gradually becomes aware (that is, conscious) of his near environment, extending it as his capacity for knowing develops. But, always, how little we know! How limited our milieu! And how constricting are the boundaries of our being! The infant finds his feet, staggers, falls, but grows in his ability to master circumstances. He grows up, leaves the family, travels, it may be all round the world, but only in limited directions and on narrow paths, for the great world will always be unknown to him. Everything he sees and learns and knows makes him all the more *conscious of what he does not know.*

Amnesia – 'forgetfulness' – is a blessed gift. Like ice on a pond, it enables mankind to walk on the surface and to skate over the depths. We call this the faculty of *repression.* Without it, life would be intolerable.

Anamnesia – 'the breaking up of forgetfulness' as it occurs in psychoanalysis – may be a devastating, excruciatingly painful experience. But it is valuable, as it leads to the release of energy and the emergence of creative potential. The *analyst* in this situation must have the qualities of faithfulness and caringness. He must be 'obstetric' – that is, 'standing by' without interfering – with the psychic strength and the required fidelity to hold the situation until the process is accomplished. Comparatively few individuals experience the past through this process of anamnesia. But all humanity builds the structure of its life on what has happened and on what has been forgotten. It may be that many skate successfully over the surface in life. But, with others, the ice is thin. When it breaks, they are in trouble. To rescue them we must be prepared to go deep into the unconscious. This may be indeed a painful process, but it brings rewards which are unknown and unavailable to the successful 'skaters'.

Unstable family relationships during infancy lead to anxiety in adult life. Cruelty and undue punishment without understanding is likely to lead to cruelty and violence in the adult. Can remedies be found? From Parliament downwards (and upwards) reformers, social workers in great variety, clergy, teachers, everywhere there are people asking the question: How do we tackle the problem of violence, delinquency, criminality, murder and social destruction? Many of the proposed solutions tackle the problem too late. More certainly the answer is that it must be tackled where it has its origin – namedly in the relationship of parent to child at the early beginnings of life. We do not need to go outside our own experience to discover resentment lingering in adult life against one or both parents. Resentment is a hostility that we have not been able to face, hostility against the parent and other adults was disallowed in the first years, punished in childhood, despaired of in the teenages – never an attitude making for acceptance in the community. Repression which we now recognize as resentment is a cruel element in all relationships, and though it has its origin in early family antagonisms, yet it spreads and is all too likely to create paranoia in adult life, that attitude in which we blame others rather than ourselves when things go wrong – always the other fellow's fault, not mine.

In order to cultivate our gardens and prepare the good soil for the seed, digging is necessary. Can we hope that in the wasteland where deprived, anxious, unfulfilled people are to be found, that also analysts will come forward willing to listen patiently so that treasure lying undiscovered, fertile soil awaiting cultivation, derelict gardens with their potential of beauty and fruitfulness, may find their gardeners with the skill and wisdom to make even the wilderness 'blossom as the rose'.

You and I as human beings are perched precariously in space, time and scale – by which we mean in size relative to the infinitesimal and the infinite. A speck of dust under the present day microscope becomes enlarged to astonish us with its size and complexity. Our planet Earth seen from the Moon diminishes to be only one small rotating sphere with others around the sun. And the Sun itself? We now know it as a point of light and energy in the galaxy, among an infinite number of galaxies, quite beyond our imagination or our comprehension.

Letting such thoughts come and go in our minds we are brought into a state of extreme humility. The Greek word *agnosis* describes it, a not-knowing enveloping us in the pride of our knowing, a realization that knowledge inevitably pushing further away the boundaries of our ignorance, is also stretching that same ignorance into infinity.

Only a century ago Freud and later Jung took up threads from earlier thinkers and began to make us wonder and speculate about the unconscious, the unknown territories of the psyche lying beneath the threshold of awareness of knowing, so that it escapes our memory.

So we ponder the question: Is now the only time we have? Contrariwise, is the 'I am' of the present day a living continuum, with nodes at conception and death of the body – is it awaiting gnosis, knowing, understanding its place in time, space and scale? Wordsworth's gift to us is his poem resonates in our memories as if we recognize the truth of it.

Our birth is but a sleep and a forgetting:
The Soul that rises with us, our life's Star,
Hath had elsewhere its setting,
And cometh from afar.
Not in entire forgetfulness
And not in utter nakedness,
But trailing clouds of glory do we come
From God, who is our home.

Quite frequently we hear thoughtful people when speaking of lovers or friends express the idea that they must have met in a former life – 'Not in entire forgetfulness do we come.' Similarly a life partner when confronted by the death experience may reassure the one remaining on earth that love is eternal and that they will meet in the hereafter. Fantasy? It may be, but who is to determine whether make-believe or satisfaction is nearer to reality?

Those of us calling ourselves analysts, who deal with our own dreams and the dreams communicated to us by others, are convinced that the dream leads us into experiences deriving from infancy (literally the pre-verbal period of life). The dream sheds light on present day experience and may even be 'precognitive' in illuminating life still to come. This reinforces the dim awareness that 'all time is present'. Analysis is a process of digging – we may dream of ourselves with a spade turning over the soil – often with the hunch that in it we shall find treasure. Indeed all those who are faithful in their analysis make the discovery that hidden gifts, unknown talents, unsuspected wisdom is *there* awaiting our willingness to dig, to explore, to relate to the deeper layers of our nature. Do we get a glimpse here of the concept of 'the deep unconscious' and 'depth analysis', deep also in the sense of forgotten memories, repressed awareness of the origins, of the whence of the ego-experience? Deep in time, considering it as a dimension of being; what about the antipodes? – the deep unconscious.

I relate here a pathetic memory which was evoked in the process of a deep analysis. My patient, Hilda, was 'only a girl' unwelcomed both before and after birth. Her mother greatly over-valued men and wished desperately she did not need to be a woman and a mother. Hilda's small brother Harry did not seem to have much value either and the two of them created fantasies in which they compensated for their rejection. Australia, they learned from their early schooling, was a place *where the settlers valued women*; females were always welcomed and there was great competition among the male population to possess and marry and wife. Another fact about Australia was of great importance – the kangaroos, inhabitants of that distant land, were extraordinary good mothers. They provided themselves with a pouch in which they carried their infants so that they need not be separated at birth. Incorporating these two items of knowledge into a game, Hilda and Harry *set out to dig to Australia*. There was a shrubbery in their garden where their activity would not be noticed. So day after day there was some progress made. How sad that they never got there!

This story goes back forty years. Hilda was faithful to the analytic process and was able to work acceptably with others who felt themselves unaccepted. Harry never reached maturity although he had a long life. Both have died and left me their story to tell you – saying to you that each child needs to be valued, to know their value, to find recognition and the comfort of close relationships. Neither Hilda nor Harry ever 'knew' in the sense of sexual fulfilment, but their 'not-knowing' comes to us as a challenge to find ways of healing, ways of bringing deprived people to find their treasure, ways of exploration so that 'Australia', where women are valued and babies held close to their mothers, may no longer be a distant land. Digging, in the sense of exploring the unconscious through dream-analysis, is not to be set aside.

The Past

Man deals with the past by forgetting, although in all probability each of us has a record imprinted with each heart beat, in some storehouse the structure of which we cannot guess. We are endowed with the capacity of ignoring that record – *ignoramus* is the Latin word for 'we do not know'.

The Future

Unknown and unknowable. How are we to deal with it? Can we ignore it? Human nature seems to demand that we anticipate. One function of the mind is to expect, to look ahead with the expectation of good or evil, reward or punishment, heaven or hell, to anticipate good time or bad, safe transit or broken bridges, the desired haven or shipwreck at sea. With hope we can see light ahead of us, with faith we are sure that life is purposeful and has a goal, that even for a ship in dark waters a way lies ahead towards the destination. Let us look back at the wake the ship has created and be sure that the way ahead is also charted. Is faith a willingness to enter into the unconscious – the darkness in which transformation is effected?

Let us remember that *psyche*, the spritual energy of man, was likened in Greek thought to the butterfly with its marvellous transitional stages: the egg; the grub which devours cabbage leaves; the cocoon where the grub's imprisonment leads to its apparent destruction; its growth into a winged creature; its emergence, its hesitant unfolding, the spreading of its wings; and at last, for the butterfly, flight into the air, the element for which it was created.

Not only individuals but mankind may today be discovering this freedom; tentatively emerging from imprisonment; slowly and cautiously opening wings; courageously taking flight in a new element, the spiritual *milieu divin* for which his Creator intended him. The old world may be passing away. But the promise is that all things will become new. Perhaps the great certainty will be 'I am spirit ... I have a body ..., and ultimately, 'I shall know even as I am known''. No longer 'ignoramus'. In the myth of Adam and Eve, when Adam *knew* Eve, new life was conceived. Cain and Abel went separate ways but Cain's life – though it was disapproved – was valued and preserved. Adam *knew* Eve and, at a crucial moment in time, *something happened.*

Mankind found new ways of life. Again, at the Annunciation, the Virgin murmured: 'What is happening? Be it unto me according to Thy Word!', and a man was born whose life incarnated the Spirit of Love.

Fear in all living creatures serves a useful purpose. It warns us of danger and it protects us from destructive influences. But fear can also serve us badly and make us anticipate evil, disaster, or destruction. We may live in anxiety, constantly projecting our fear onto the unknown, lacking confidence in life's purpose, and losing sight of the underlying structure which we may call the love of God.

Is the future determined by chance and by accident? Or is there a man on the bridge who steers the ships through the dark waters of the pathless ocean? Has life a structure? Is there a *telos* (the Greek word meaning 'end') in the sense of an aim, a goal, or a fulfilment? Dimensions stretch to infinity, beyond our vision, towards an end. As our minds mature through experience, we become less and less willing to use the word 'chance' and we may come to believe or to know that there is no such thing as an 'accident'. Everything is ordered. Again, we may think of T.S. Eliot in *Four Quartets* with his vision that the whole fabric of time may be contained in the one creative moment, the everlasting *now*.

History tells us of the rise and fall of nations and dynasties. We thought it told us of the growth of wisdom and perhaps even of the conquest of love by hate. Then Hitler arose and within him came a new awareness of evil which demanded that each of us should ask in our own psyche: 'Can it be me?'

'Ignoramus'. We do not know. But, in the evolution of life, it is certain that *something is happening*. We are not stuck and confined forever in the Alpha of our beings for, ahead of us with its attracting energy, lies the Omega, the goal of our being.

Expectation and desire are closely linked, for example, in wishful thinking. Wanting. Wishing. Desiring. Can we go a step further and expect to get what we want? What we ask for? What we pray for? We can lose nothing by trusting the hunch that somehow good will be the final goal of ill, even if our reason insists on the uncertainty of that. Hope and faith are spiritual qualities, eternal values. Through all uncertainties they re-assure us. Pessimism and despair may suggest that God is absent but hope and faith assert that He is ever present. Life's task may well be to keep an awareness of that Presence. Again, look at Pope John Paul I. We were told that he was smiling as he died. Absolute certainty sustained him as he perceived, in that moment in time, that death is not the end of life's road but rather the gateway to life's fulfilment. Each of us can say with conviction: 'I am spirit ... I have a body ... I happen to have a body.' The body is disposable but the spirit, pure energy, is indestructible. It changes, it matures, it takes new forms. And, always, in the life of the spirit, *something is happening*.

Hunches ... uncertainties ... Can we trust them and build upon them? Charles Darwin, who died just before I was born, had a hunch on which he built the great Theory of Evolution. In it, he added his intuitive observation and reason. His intuition showed him that life is a continuous process, an emergence, an unfolding – like the growth of an oak tree from its acorn. The great sciences of biology, zoology, ecology, and even psychology owe their structure to the insight and wisdom of this intuitive personality. He stimulated others who, linking their discoveries with his, opened doors to knowledge that still effect all our lives today.

One of the great postulates of the teaching of evolution is that *ontogeny repeats phylogeny*. By ontogeny, the individual in his growth relives and repeats the development of the human race. In 280 days (10 lunar months), a single cell – the zygote – becomes a human being. Humanity has taken countless aeons to develop from the origin of life in chthonic matter to the men and women of today who are endowed with understanding and are capable of developing their intelligence beyond our imagination.

Is all time contained in the present? Past and future as well as *now*? Is evolution taking place as our clocks mark the hours and our calendars the years? The human race can only change and develop through change in the individual. 'Significant variations', who are of value for the survival and the benefit of the race, are occurring *now* just as they have occurred throughout the long history of humanity. The acceleration of this process, however, is greater today than ever before. Today our school children have a knowledge and a comprehension of facts that were quite unknown to our grandparents. With the stimulus of enormously increasing knowledge, it is probable that Man's mind is opening to grasp new dimensions from which again fresh conceptions will develop. Meantime, let us be content to not-know, but to be part of this vast, mysterious change.

14.

Old Age

The early years of my life were spent in the Victorian age, and the poetry of Robert Browning fell into my hands in my early teens. His philosophy has greatly influenced my life ever since.

Listen to what he said to a girl of fifteen:

Grow old along with me!
The best is yet to be,
The last of life, for which the first was made:
Our times are in His hand,
Who saith: 'A whole I planned,
Youth shows but half; trust God: see all nor be afraid!'

An anonymous writer spoke to me, apparently fortuitously in a Thought for the Day Calendar when I was in my early forties and his words have shed light on my path ever since:

We should know we are getting old *not* by the frailty of the body but by the strength and creativity of the spirit.

Half of my days lay behind me and I was not dissatisfied with what had been achieved in the development of skills through this period of growth – education, medical and surgical hospital work, marriage, child-bearing and child rearing. When this 'thought' came into my hands I had embarked on the process of psychoanalysis which was so radically to change my life. I was now *to grow old* but this must lie ahead of me as a time of fulfilment, growth to maturity not decay, a time for which the earlier life experience had been a preparation.

I was unaware of Jung's psychology in these days but I now accept his teaching that there is a watershed in our lives, an attainment which we may liken to a mountain ridge. We look back and see something of what our life has been in terms of son or daughter; the road behind us has not been without its rough and difficult stretches but here we are, surviving, able to assess something at last of life's achievements. What lies ahead? We are getting old. 'Too old at forty' was a slogan of that time and it was quite usual to meet men and women anticipating their future with dismay. In some cases this was more or less tempered with the thought of escape from drudgery. It was fairly common to meet men looking forward at a time when they could play golf all day and every day, but, as these days approached this must have seemed less and less desirable, more so if their physical condition was deteriorating.

About this time an incident occurred through which I saw there were optimistic ways of looking ahead. I can remember myself at the front door of the house where we were then living, bidding farewell to a friend whom I knew to be at least ten years older than myself. 'I am just going to a singing lesson' she said as she bade me farewell. My reaction was one of surprise mingled with pity: 'Poor old thing, in her fifties.' She turned to say that she felt this was, or should be, a creative period in a woman's life. Child bearing and child rearing make great *physical* demands from which a woman can now stand back. Looking ahead she may well find that it is not impossible to take up some activity through which she will gain spiritual (psychological) satisfaction, perhaps in the realm of music or art. Bergson has told us that the new-born child is a bundle of possibilities. May this also be true as times of re-birth come into our lives?

The incident – in real life – occurred at the door and we may well remember how 'opportunity' gives us a reminder that *porta*, the door, will open to us if we are not imprisoned by outworn patterns of the past, nor by fear anticipating frustration in the future.

To some of us life is very rich in opportunity. There are many doors whether we open them or not, but to all of us the message comes 'Seek and ye shall find'. Knock at the door. We must prepare ourselves for this part of life that lies on the other aspect of the watershed. Every skill acquired, every tool whose use is mastered, every craft seen as a possible means of creative expression – all will bear fruit in the later years of life reassuring us that 'I can' sees us on life's way hopefully and courageously. We must keep in mind how God spoke to the patriarchs in their old age – 'Only be strong and work, for I am with you, saith the Lord of Hosts.'

Shakespeare wrote *King Lear* towards the end of his creative life, and through Edgar he gives a message to humanity which we must all accept.

> Men must endure
> Their going hence, even as their coming hither;
> Ripeness is all.

We learn in old age to accept the fact that the body is disposable, and to learn, with more conviction, that the spirit never dies; we may say 'I am spirit, I happen to have a body.' Maturity is what matters. As fruit matures it scatters its seed and this again falling on to good earth grows and reproduces 'First the blade, then the ear, and then the full corn on the ear' – the recurring cycle of life. But ripeness is all, immature seed perishes. Till we come to the watershed the fact of death may be accepted *by the mind* but it is rejected, much less welcomed, until we see the road stretching out to the beyond far beyond body death.

We must keep in mind that it is through the maturing of the spirit when we lay hold on the awareness that we are called to the creative, to become conscious that our ripeness, that is our fruit-bearing, enriches humanity and matters to Life as a whole. Old age bears in on us with the message that the body must die. More than that, it gives us an awareness that the spirit, our psyche, is *not* liable to death – but is given transformation and a new life. Let us look again at the symbol of the psyche – the Greek word for butterfly. The egg, lying dormant, matures into the grub, the caterpillar. In its maturity, having eaten enough cabbage leaf, it creates its cocoon where it disintegrates and grows its new body with wings. Close folded in the cocoon with no obvious way out, we can imagine a situation of great fear – no known future, only darkness, discomfort. But something is happening – emergence – the spreading of the wings, new life quite unpredictable to the caterpillar. In old age the cocoon must be developing a crack, light is shed, and hope, not despair, heralds tomorrow. In some cases illness or accident dramatically changes our outlook and perspective, but more usually it is through a gradual process that we accustom ourselves to the certainty that our physical life ends but that spirit cannot.

The ageing process seems to have in itself an awakening of hope, gradually increasing to certainty that loss of our body in death is not the end of the road but only a gateway to the beyond.

Talking of the anamnesia occurring through analytic work, calling it 'the breaking up of forgetfulness', we see that such a process occurs frequently in old age, with strange possibilities activating themselves which are not easily dismissed. At such time death of the body comes to be not only accepted but welcomed. When St Paul writes that this state is 'much better' (since we are with Christ), this must be a tremendous understatement but still we can hold on to it till the full awareness of what is happening comes true in our lives 'in the hereafter' – that is when we reach the stretch of road beyond the gate of death.

Without death, life would be unendurable to ourselves and others. 'I wish I were dead' and 'I wish he/she were dead' come from the depth of our being which is linked with the instinctual nature that unites us to all creatures who live and die. A Russian short story called *When Death took a Holiday* pictures a nightmarish eternity of ill-health and bad relationships. In the Hindu translation of the verse in which St John tells us that Jesus says 'In my Father's house are many mansions', the word used is *basha.* A traveller on India's great hill roads calls the basha the 'Dak-bungalow' – a place where he rests overnight, is fed, and goes on his way. So in our journey towards God there are many stretches of the road, many gates through which we must pass, many resting places. Perhaps we can not only endure but welcome each stretch as it comes. Like Edgar in *King Lear* can we *know* that ripening is what matters on each stage of the journey? Like Browning may we have the conviction that youth sees but half and that we need not fear to face the whole?

Again we can have great thankfulness that when the outworn clothing, which is the body, is disposed of and dies, we are not left naked but given a new body, perhaps now that of a winged creature, at home in the world of the spirit – symbolized by the butterfly stretching its wings in a hitherto undiscovered element, the air. While they are folded in the cocoon, we cannot understand their use, but now opening, spreading, they bring us into a life hitherto unimagined – and in their life is fulfilment and creativity.

A few millenia have passed since 'Three score years and ten' were cited as a normal lifetime. Man, maybe more foolish nowadays than he was then, eats the wrong sort of food, inventing tins and tin openers, refining the grains and so ridding them of essential vitamin content, destroying by cooking vegetables better eaten raw. Civilization does not seem to have made us wise in the matter of diet, although there too something is happening and in some circles we are again honouring Mother Nature and her gifts, which may well help to prolong life. Civilization has provided us also, with an artificial limit to a working life: women become pensioners at the age of sixty and men five years later – why? To make room for the younger folk whom unemployment threatens and frustrates. Remembering again that at birth each of us is 'a bundle of possibilities', can we use this belief to prepare us for the seventh and subsequent decades so that in them as well as in youth we may find our creativity and need not dread unemployment?

A prescription against ageing given to me fifty years ago might be helpful: 'This year and each subsequent year attempt to achieve three things. Make a new friend, acquire a new skill, learn a new language.' Even if only one of these is acted on it will delay the onset of ageing. You may notice they refer to heart, head and hand – friendship awakens love, language acquisition bestirs the mind, and even ageing hands can be used to weave or at least to spin the wool, to draw, or better still to paint or find other ways of making pictures, to write. Suppose that today you begin to work at your autobiography – it will be surprisingly interesting! What about recording your dreams and finding someone who will help you to discover meaning in this activity? It may well remove the blockage that is denying you the courage to step out of your inability to work and to create and give you fresh impetus to get going on some possible project. I am again, you will recognize, on my favourite topic – *involve yourself in awareness of the unconscious.*

Let us go back to consider the question of why old age overcomes some people in their sixties or even earlier, while we have others in their ninth or even tenth decade still able to live happily, not too dependent on others, able still to make friends and to be open to new knowledge. What is their secret? Probably one answer is in heredity; they belong to a long-living stock. They chose their parents well. Closely related to this is probably an element of expectation. How important that word is few people fully realize. The idea of auto-suggestion became prevalent and gained great popularity between the wars before many people – even the highly educated – had become conscious of Freud. In auto-suggestion we are deliberately using the unconscious, feeding into it (if we use it wisely) ideas of better meat. Coué's formula 'Day by day in every way I am getting better and better' seems a bit childish today, but to the crowds who thronged his clinic at Nancy in Alsace, *it worked.* We may well train ourselves to use some such formula. Mothers at bedtime with a sick child can murmur 'All better in the morning' so that the expectation of healing takes place in sleep.

The anxious mother who foresees further trouble, expecting things to go wrong, handicaps her child's life, and maternal anxiety may well be thought of as one of the factors operating in her offspring even in their old age. We are fortunate if we have kept up the good habit of expecting that we shall be quite well tomorrow – or at least getting better.

It is strange and sad to see people deliberately shortening their expectation of health and longevity with alcohol, cigarettes, drugs of one sort and another. Death wishes must be affecting them strongly.

From the Jewish psalter we have reference to the faithful whose lives are like trees planted by the river – indeed this symbolism occurs several times in the Bible. With our roots in the water we are likely to survive and to bear fruit. In psychological language this may well mean 'Dig deep: water flows underground'. We must not be content to live life on the surface but must learn to explore the depths. At the deeper levels we lose the expectancy that evil will triumph over good but rather acquire more and more certainty that in so far as the body is undertaking work for others it is likely to keep alive.

Arrogance over length of days is stupid and senseless but we can be glad when age brings wisdom and does not take from us the ability to help others, to encourage them still to contribute to the world's needs. 'When we dread labour, then only are we old.' The renewal of youth is evident when we can say 'Not I'. Not the ego with its mask putting a good face on its weakness, but the 'Not I' taught to us in Paul's writings – 'Not I but Christ'. Young or old? It matters not at all – what does matter is that Christ's energy should work in us. Then as live wires we carry what we are given far further than we could ask or imagine.

15.

The Emergence of Human Potential

Consulting the dictionaries about the origin of our English word *potential* we learn that it is derived from the Latin verb *potere* – to be able. Two subsidiary meanings of the word that are given are interesting and stimulate our thought. Firstly, 'the head of a crutch'. Does this indicate that the crutch enables the cripple (powerless, impotent) to walk, by uniting him to Mother Earth? Another meaning is: 'The work done between infinity and the unit of mass or electricity.' Infinity – the ultimate source of energy: the individual unit of life – you and I at our jobs. Do we as 'potential' stand just there, between the source and the point at which the work awaits accomplishment?

There is a feeling of expectancy about the word; something awaits fulfilment. Do you get the picture of someone lying abed, knowing there is work to be done but unable to rise and set about the task? 'Can do' – yes, but the willingness may be dormant, chained to the bed, at the mercy of impotence. A bell rings. Aware of the summons he is able to rise. It was what he needed – a demand from something outside himself – and he is now in command of his energy, his ability, his potency.

Is life like that? Are you also asleep, lying abed, awaiting the call to action? Are you perhaps envying one of your friends? 'How I wish I had his energy' you perhaps say. The energy is there but you and I need the stimulus to awaken it, to set it on its journey from the source to the point of usefulness.

From time to time in everyday experience we meet a man or woman who elicits from us a feeling of wonder, as sensing their vitality we recognize what we sometimes call 'a live wire'. Sometimes such people have a great vehemence of bodily activity, but in others it is a stillness through which we are aware that energy is being transmitted.

They are people who are living out the fundamental injunction of *life* to man: *TAKE-HOLD-GIVE*. There is no accidental, fortuitous process involved. They are not people who from time to time take thought about getting their 'batteries recharged', but rather those who know what God's continuing Presence means in their lives and want to know how they can establish this contact and gain a permanent inflow. We again listen to Moses, accepting what he had demanded of God, hearing the words 'My Presence shall go with thee and I shall give thee rest.' No *statis*, this 'rest', but an absence of anxiety, a sureness of the goal as we seek the way.

Electricity has, I suppose, been there since the Universe was created. How strange that only in this century has it been harnessed to serve man's need of heat and light and power! In my own childhood homes were lit by candles and paraffin lamps, or in towns by gas. I well remember a party where we danced in an Edinburgh house and were first aware that by 'pressing a button' we could turn light on and off – a strange miracle in those days! This was in the year 1900. A few years later, in 1903, as a medical student, I was attending lectures in physics and learning something of the harnessing of this great power by Faraday, Galvani, Marconi, Madame Curie and others. The first motor cars were made in Germany the year I was born (1885) but they were still rarities in Scotland in my college days and electric tramcars came into use much later.

I must not linger over the way electricity has revolutionized transport, so that 'horse-power' has become obsolete, only the word remaining to keep us in touch with the commonly-used source of energy as this century began. The media (a word unknown at that time) developed apace in the second and third quarters of the twentieth century, greatly dependent on the service of electrical power. Electricity, then, is now part of the basis of our bodily existence.

But it is also a symbol of psychic energy– the connecting link between the physical and the spiritual. This symbolism is seen in our use of the word 'potential.' We talk of 'electrical potential', and of 'human potential.'

When we use the word 'potential' as a noun it evokes images of controlled force – the seed, for instance, like the acorn, with its possibility of growth into a great oak tree. Again we can think of steam under pressure, or waves off the Hebridean coasts, their potential released, their power turning engine wheels or great electrical dynamos, infinite in their adaptability for use as energy. I am reminded of Salter's 'ducks', waiting to make available to mankind the great energy of the ocean as it breaks upon the shore. Again we can envisage a reservoir of water dammed up behind great embankments and needing to be channelled for usefulness. Unchannelled, it may burst through its limiting structures, causing untold damage and devastation. Visualize the Dead Sea – and remember the bitterness of its waters. Unchannelled, they overflow the banks, harming all the vegetation they touch as the flood spreads. The desert land, the infertile plains, spread farther afield, affected by the bitter water. Can we see the analogy to human energy?

For we human beings also have, locked up in our individual psyche, energies awaiting release. Within the last few decades, something very intimate, and extremely relevant to our lives has come to light. This is the fact demonstrated by Harold Burr of Yale University, that every cell of the human body has a charge of electro-magnetic force. This means that you and I have in our bodies an immense storehouse of energy which we constantly employ and which we never cease to pour out into the environment. Whither? We can ask the question, but so far the answer can only be that we do not know to what infinity it is reaching. Our hunch is that it cannot be destroyed, but possibly, going full circle, comes again into our lives. The ultimate source we call God. But a great deal of our 'potential' of psychic energy is not realized.

In community and society there are untapped resources sorely needed in the world as it develops and its population grows. A story told two thousand years ago gave us the word *talent*, teaching us of each man's personal endowment and encouraging us to use it to the full. The unused talent – that is the undeveloped potential – sent its owner to hell. Today the gift that gets no expression, the talent that lies undeveloped, causes its owner untold suffering. We may truly say it sends him to hell. If outlet is not provided for the energy of steam the result is disastrous: the rising pressure destroys the container, the boiler bursts. This relates to a very primitive fear that many of us remember as children – the fear that the cistern will overflow and overwhelm us. One little boy is said to have always ended his bedtime prayer with 'And please God don't let the boiler burst.' We can interpret this as fear of our own unused, unchannelled potential and remind ourselves that 'Ultimately all fear is endopsychic.' We project it on to situations we don't understand. Other people's anger, the darkness of the coal-cellar, many mysteries provide panic. Withdrawing the projections, we must ask: Can it be me? *Can it be my own unused potential* that is so threatening my very existence?

Before his Passion Jesus used a word 'inasmuch' and set us visualizing his 'little brethren' who are hungry, thirsty, naked, isolated, prisoners and sick folk. Urging us to realize our potential power and wealth he asks us to get in touch with them and to realize that our giving will encounter the divine hand that takes again. The circle is completed, a new level of existence is reached and man enters into his kingdom.

The energy of the universe, with which we are in touch through our psyche, is essentially creative. It is always seeking its way into mankind. Primitive man in the caves of the Pyrenees, and his brother the bushman of the Kalahari, both depicted the animals they hunted with great beauty of line. After many years this gift matured and men such as Leonardo and Rembrandt appeared. In music too the notes on primitive pipe or harp developed into the themes of Mozart and the symphonies of Beethoven. So the liberation and expression of psychic energy – of each man's 'talent' is of immense importance both for the individual and for mankind in general. When the gift is expressed something happens. When buried, not only the talent itself is lost but its capacity for development, growth, complexity and usefulness is buried and comes to nothing.

But can a lost and buried talent be recovered? Very primitive animals like lizards, losing a limb, have the capacity to grow it again. Man does not regrow lost fingers and toes, but the buried talent has its potential of regrowth. In the spirit – the psyche – nothing dies, and the repressed, underdeveloped gift, finding opportunity and freed from repression, takes on new life.

At first in my work as an analyst I was surprised and delighted by seeing this emergence of creativity. The work of psycho-analysis was at that time thought of as a therapy – a cure for sick, abnormal people – a treatment of neurotic illness, that is ill-health in its many manifestations caused by anxiety. Anxiety – St Paul called it 'the spirit of fear' – is the attachment of fear inappropriately to certain events of circumstances because its original cause and occasion has been lost in the unconscious, repressed, forgotten. Analysis involves *anamnesia* – literally 'the breaking up of forgetfulness' – and in recovering, remembering, reliving it may be, the original fear-laden incident – relief is obtained, the conditioning tie is broken, and one quantum of our free-floating anxiety is released.

Analysis has still this function – the treatment of anxiety-ridden people, who exist crippled, uneasy, impoverished, hesitant in their living, terrified of dying and suffering the many indignities of bodily illness. This relief from anxiety is indeed the measure of the method's success, which is considerable and to be relied on, and it is sufficient reason for its practice. I have already said, however, that concomitantly with release from fear and anxiety *something else happens*. With the return to consciousness of the repressed material, creativity is released: the energy of the psyche surges into life seeking outlet. I remember very vividly how the realization of this process came to me.

In the years between 1929, when I entered the field of analysis, and 1939 when the Davidson Clinic was established, I had begun to see my life work as deliverance from fear, in myself and others, into a life of creative love and sanity. My first patients astonished me, as I mentioned above, by a sudden uprush of activity. They began to paint, to weave, to write poetry, to sing. Something was happening to them. Hidden gifts emerging, creative energy was replacing the fear that had kept them depressed, physically sick, the victims of inertia. The parable of the talents took on new meaning for me. I realized that when the talent is unused, people do live in hell: there is no need to send them there! Even in the late 1920s before the Davidson Clinic was established, I had work rooms attached to my consulting room with Hilda, an ex-patient, as craft worker in charge. She encouraged old arthritic fingers to weave, as well as eliciting great skill and achievement from the younger people. Great happiness and activity was engendered in the small groups which gathered there to paint, to weave, and to make things. Hilda herself became a new person as her work with others gave her great creative outlet. I began to understand why the Dead Sea is dead – it takes and holds, but does not give again. It has its inflow but not its outflow. Our Lord told us we must give bread to the hungry, give water to the thirsty, give clothing to the naked, go ourselves to the prisoner and the sick persons. In so giving we keep the life-giving creative libido always flowing, filling and emptying our lives. We then know ourselves as channels – channels between the source and the 'little ones' – the least of Christ's brethren whose need we can supply.

Is the tremendous potential of the unconscious awaiting conduits – channels through which it can flow? *Libido* – the word used for psychic energy – means 'flow.' When there is no flow then we are depressed, feel ourselves useless, unwilling and unable to give, unlovable and unloved, as if the tap controlling the energy had been turned off – no flow, no energy, no libido available. Many people know all too well this condition of depression for which they seek psychiatric treatment. It is not however to this extremity of suffering that Gurdjieff refers when he says mankind is asleep and urges us to buy an alarm clock or its psychic equivalent, or to find other means of awakening. He is stating rather that our lives are dull and uncreative, our minds inert and stagnant. It is as if, poverty-stricken, the libido drips and falters instead of maintaining a steady flow 'irrigating the flowerbeds', making life desirable, full of love and joy and peace.

Is man's true function to carry this energy, deriving from the very ground of our being, into society, to all men and women, so often half dead, lethargic, unawakened? Does the symbolism of the smoking flax apply to this world of smouldering society? Do we need our spark to be fanned into a flame? Does this happen when any one of us is vitalised by contact with the divine flame, ever alight in the ground of our being? Jesus was surely aware of this when he said: 'I am come that they may have life – the life more abundant.' We are apt to recoil from the suggestion that our individual lives may have such possibilities. What an inflation of a human personality! Recoiling, we say again and again 'Not I. Not I, but Christ in me the hope of glory', and call to mind Paul's teaching 'Out of this Infinite Glory may he give us the power (energy) through the Spirit that the hidden self may grow strong.' Again is it not to the 'live wire' that Paul refers when he writes – 'whose power (energy) working in us does infinitely more than we can ask *or imagine*'?

At times we lose contact with the Source, but, if we wait, we shall find it again. In Christ we have the light, the flame that has lightened every man coming into the world, awakening us that we too may be light. Through the self, the Hidden Self of St Paul's prayer for his converts, the *Atman* of the Vedas, a place is provided in the psyche for the Christ to live in our hearts. Then we become living conduits, live wires, ready to transmit the energy, where it is needed in the lives of men – so co-operating in the divine purpose that mankind should awaken to its creative destiny.

In the light of these experiences we must ask whether religion and psychology are closely related disciplines, interdependent, elucidating complementary teachings, hypotheses and beliefs. In studying *depth psychology*, i.e. the exploration of unconscious processes, we come upon the very stuff out of which our lives have grown. For some a relatively firm foundation of a secure family, a protected home where kindness and understanding prevailed rather than harsh discipline, angry responses or rejection of their childish weaknesses. These latter, with the terrible suffering of the frightened child who has dissolute parents, a broken home, no support for routine and discipline, create the anxious insecure people who break down in time of crisis, who take refuge in addiction to drugs or alcohol. They in their turn become unreliable parents so that from generation to generation the pattern is repeated – insecurity, anxiety, breakdown. It may be, and today all too frequently is, that the suffering child in due course becomes delinquent, criminal, a murderer, the enemy of society, the destroyer of security, bringing fear and terror into other people's lives, filling our institutes for unwanted children, filling also our prisons and hospitals, and, in old age, infiltrating society with their helpless inefficiency and dependence instead of with strength and reliability and helpfulness to the oncoming generations.

In face of all this, must we be hopeless and conclude that there must be inevitable disaster? Surely not, surely there's always the Way, but can we get back on to it? Can we find the Tao, the Way, can we listen to the voice, a voice that will undoubtedly speak to us saying, 'This is the Way, this is the Way'?

Let us look then at what is happening today in the world of analysis. There are increasingly numbers of people who have had what we think of as deep analysis, perhaps attending an analyst once, twice or even more often in a week, perhaps continuing their analysis over not weeks or months, but years. We think of them outwardly as deeply analysed people and they undoubtedly have access to a region of the psyche, the deep unconscious which is in contact with the Source. And let us call it the Source with a capital S. These people speak with authority. Are they arrogant to speak with authority? Or rather can we say, 'No, they have the prerogative to speak with authority because they are being informed, nourished, illuminated from the deeper layers of the psyche, of the unconscious, of knowing. Surely an example of the prerogative of authority is recorded in the Gospels where it is said that Jesus spoke 'with authority and not as the Scribes.' The Scribes were repeating the old laws – they were the textbooks of the time (and today we are overwhelmed by such textbook technicians) – while Jesus spoke 'with authority,' that is with direct access to the wisdom of the unconscious.

The people who have experienced the unconscious processes through analysis are having a tremendous influence in the world, in writing, in drama, in art, in music. What they have learned in the depths of their own being is coming through to a much bigger public, a much wider range of humanity. Everywhere throughout the world the influence, this leaven is spreading itself amongst others who are writing or working for the enlightenment of Mankind. But the teaching of Freud and Jung do not only come to us directly through analysed people. Through so many different channels, others have received the teaching and are using it to influence society. Take as an example Laurens van der Post, and what he is doing, what his stories are doing for us in so widespread a way, so deeply religious, so deeply aware of the mind of the primitive of whom he writes enchantingly. Think how he describes the men and women of the Kalahari in touch with nature.

And this example is multiplied many many times in our world just now. People may not have heard of Jung and may deny the validity of the Freudian teaching, yet how deeply their lives have undoubtedly been affected. I suppose every criminal court is fortunate if in it somebody at least has a clue as to the causation of delinquency, of what it is that brings those criminals into a state of stress, isolation and anti-social behaviour. I am told that just as we no longer allow the word 'criminal' to be attached to children. Many people indeed are trying to get away from the word 'criminal' for all ages and to see the criminal as a person in distress, as a person in difficulty, as someone who has had his or her life messed up at some stage or other and is therefore cut off from the Source, the source of healing, of understanding, of caring and of love for their fellow Man. Love is being replaced by hate and violence.

Long ago when Christianity first came to the Roman Empire, the Emperor Constantine urged one of the teachers of the day to destroy all idols, but one wise philosopher stood up to Constantine and said, 'In the face of so great a mystery are there not many roads to God?' And this we must keep today; we must not be arrogant. There is 'The Way, the Truth and the Life' that our Lord claimed, but when we read in St John's gospel, 'No Man cometh unto the Father but by me,' we can see it as meaning that there are many, many ways to the Father, but all of them are the Christ ways. It is not an arrogant claiming of the one Way, but it is the claiming that there is the Christ's spirit in every Way.

In my childhood and youth we were sending missionaries to the East to spread the Christian gospel, and today, strangely, they have nearly all been recalled. Now streaming in from India, China, Tibet, Japan and Thailand too, we get the different schools teaching us the ways of meditation, other ways of approaching the great Source.

These paths of Eastern meditation lead to the discovery within oneself of the deeper levels of being, of the Source of energy and of all goodness. This is strangely akin to the unconscious we seek through analysis. My friend Tew Bunnag tells me that in deep Vipassana Meditation, a form of Buddhism that comes to us from Thailand, material emerges from the unconscious in a very similar way to the *anamnesia* of analysis. Anamnesia (as we have seen) means 'the break-up of forgetfulness' and the meditator is flooded with childish feelings and memories needing to be understood and assimilated.

Have the saints in Christian meditation also made the same discoveries? Is Christ in all these ways, the Christ spirit? I feel the answer must be 'yes.' Many ways but one Christ, many ways but one message and the message is 'I am the Way'. The message of Christ is 'The Way, the Truth, the Life.' Religion and psychology in their depth touch the same level, the Source, the ground of our being. It is time that we have the courage to see this and to bring them together. In recent times, not only from the East, but also from the West there are the Ways. There are always new developments in California. Ten years ago we had Encounter and the work that was done in Esalen. Also we think of the development of Wilhelm Reich's work which is called Bio-energetics. Through these ways other developments are constantly taking place. There is Gestalt, Intensive Journal, Transactional Analysis, all the various schools of Clinical Psychology. Some of them we accept, others we are unsure whether to accept or reject. But how much does it matter? Are there not many ways to God and many many people who must find the Way? They do not always choose the same way and yet the message in all these ways is the Christ Spirit, there is a taking of us to God.

Recently I was interviewed on behalf of the BBC about my life and work as an analyst. In response to this I received a a great number of letters. All of them touched me deeply. Some told of 'the opening of a door' in their lives through an apparently chance listening to a radio programme. But many others bring one up against this terrible problem of the so-called 'hopeless case.' Yet in my lifetime I have learnt to ask this question, 'Is there such a thing as a hopeless patient, a hopeless case, or are there only hopeless doctors?' And so what are the possibilities for those people who write from a distance telling how severely crippled they are, how closely imprisoned they have become by their symptoms. Again and again we must be aware and help them to recognize that there are many ways of healing and many roads to God.

Some of the writers give a very sad report of all that has happened to them in the course of their treatment for their disabilities. A great deal of psychological ill-health, this psychological distress is commuted into physical illness. The psyche and soma are not separate entities, the psyche expresses itself in the soma and the soma in the psyche. We quote Browning again: 'Not soul helps body more than body soul.' Listen to the body language, be aware of what the body is saying and your psychological awareness will deepen.

Are there such things as 'hopeless cases'? In other words, are we working alone as individuals in this great field of physical and psychological illness? As therapists we must be increasingly aware of the source of healing and of its work in so many different ways throughout the world today. Let us turn again to the Good Book. We go right back now to the teaching that came millenia before Christ, to Moses, and here we know that the word spoken was, 'I am the Lord that healeth thee.' Healing is not a thing of drugs, of modern medicine, of modern shock therapy, even of modern analysis. What is healing? Healing must be a direct relationship to the healing power which we postulate is found in the deep unconscious. So we talk of the Source of our healing, of the Source of all healing. (Let's always use the capital S.) Let's see it as something that in a way we have to keep, as a matter of holiness. Holiness, wholeness, sanity, sanctity – not separate conceptions but a conception of that which is possible in every human life.

When we say the words of the Lord's Prayer, 'Thy will be done' we so often shrug our shoulders and say, 'Oh yes, I suppose so, I suppose so. God's will or whatever it involves, suffering, death, relief from life, I suppose we have to acknowledge it.' But is there another way of looking at the will of God? Is the will of God not also allied to the love of God? And can we not take it that the will of God is always for the total good of Mankind? Can we come to the will of God and issue in wholeness, in health, in healing? We remember the word *libido* again, the flow, and throughout the Bible the idea of the flow of the river – of the water of life – is taught right way back in the Old Testament and again in the Gospel where our Lord said, 'I am the living water; whoever drinks this water will never thirst. It will be within him as a spring of water welling up into life everlasting.' So we have this water not only for our own healing, but it is welling up within us. Is it available for the healing of others? It is so great a temptation to think of hopeless cases, of hopeless patients. The task must be to make this living water that wells up within us available for the healing of others who perhaps we shall never see and yet who appeal to us for help.

I have a feeling that for those of us who are called to be healers, the most important thing is that we should be in close relationship with this Source within ourselves, as only through the flow of life in our lives can we direct that flow into the lives of others. Is it arrogant to suppose that some of us are chosen to teach perhaps 'with authority,' to find ourselves in touch with truth and of course always a new generation finds new truths. We should be thankful and glad to know that our truth too will become obsolete or will fade out, but that the next generation, and subsequent generations, if they keep in touch with the depths, with the wisdom of the ages, will always be in touch with the one Source but in new ways. And although the Tao, the Way takes a fresh direction it leads us to the same end. What is that end? It is fullness of life, the *Omega*, for once life is united with the great Source it will increasingly give its wisdom to humanity. Listen again to Paul's words, 'Glory be to him whose power working in us does infinitely more than we can ask or imagine.'

Sending this message and the energy to outer world, let us be quite sure that it is the 'Not I' who is speaking – that it is something infinitely more, using me – the 'I' – as a channel, as a 'live wire'. Sure enough, the message is going out and *something is happening.*

Epilogue: The Lord's Prayer

The disciples of Jesus called him 'Lord' and he said they did well to call him so. It is recorded that they begged him to teach them to pray as John the Baptist, his fore-runner, had taught his disciples. Today, when this prayer is used – and indeed not a moment out of the twenty-four hours but someone, somewhere, is using these words – let us turn our faces to him again who is our Lord and learn anew how he would have us pray. We may remember learning it at our Mother's knee and finding it difficult to understand. Children are still learning it today. A great chain of devout people round the globe are using these words, some it may be thoughtlessly, but we can make it our endeavour to join with them all, not only using the *words* but seeking the understanding and making every endeavour to bring its teaching into our lives today. Shall we not only say the Lord's Prayer, but pray to God using the words that our Lord has taught us.

The spirit of the prayer – can it be lived as well as spoken? Are we seeking its fulfilment in all our relationships? Is its significance increasing as we use it and meditate upon it or has it become mere repetition? Undoubtedly when we use these petitions thoughtfully and reverently ever weighing their meaning, meditating with fresh attention and interest daily, a great deal opens up in our thinking and we feel afresh our unity with him who said 'When you pray, say 'Our Father." Our awareness of the meaning of worship increases.

Let us look at it again together using the version given in Matthew's gospel and still commonly used in all our churches today. (Matt. 6, v.9-13)

Our Father which art in heaven

The very first word of the prayer awakens a feeling of unity. There is no *I, me, mine* only *we, us, our.* So *our* Father – we summon the brotherhood and gather all together under the sheltering wings: those who are near to us and need our prayers, others scattered over the globe; those who have gone ahead of us and are free from earthly bonds – we come together in this prayer.

Father, source of our being, ultimate reality, the creative energy from which all derives – yet also *Abba* father, the giver of all good gifts and the giver of the holy spirit. Abba in the Aramaic is the child's name – 'Dad'. In the two-ness of this conception of God can we find truth? The infinite spirit, *not* to be found either in the temple nor on the mountain, not in the church buildings nor it may be in the Church itself, but spirit to be worshipped by the spirit in man – found by all who seek to worship Him in spirit and in truth. (John 10: v.21-24)

Our Father Then all men are brothers and unless we love the brother whom we see and know, how can we love the father whom we neither see nor know – invisible, intangible, unknowable? The answer is we love Him because He first loved us, He begets us in love and His love begets our love. *Our Father – not 'My Father'* – can ego-centricity die? Can we relinquish the *you and I* in favour of the *we*? With all men everywhere can we become God-created, ever seeking His face, waiting, watching, listening? 'As the eyes of the servants *wait* on the hand of the masters so our eyes *wait* on the Lord our God.'

Let us remember how the infinitely small sperm of the earthly father lives in his child, carrying the inheritance, and that the recognition of father-child relationship comes through the *likeness* to the father. Are we *like* our Father?

The word brother has its origin in bread which is cognate with breast – brothers are breast-sharers, they share the parenthood.

God is incarnate, Jesus tells us, in the least of his brothers, in the least of God's children, and that *in as much* as we give and take with these suffering little ones we are giving and taking with Him and ultimately with the Father.

In this teaching of unity Jesus used the symbolism of the vine. 'I am the vine; you are the branches' – the same sap flowing in our lives as in His. 'Unless the branch abides in the vine – keeps its oneness – it cannot bear fruit. No more can we unless we keep our relationship in Christ's spirit.

If we 'abide' – keep our relationship – we shall bear much fruit – the fruits of the spirit. St Paul enumerates them: Love, joy, peace, patience, kindness, goodness, faithfulness, gentleness and self-control. Let us remember the Cathars' beautiful prayer:

> Grant us to know as Thou knowest and to love as Thou lovest since we are not of this world as Thou art not of this world.

Is it asking for increase in our consciousness and capacity for love? God has come into the world as the spirit of love, the caring spirit, the holy spirit, the Christ. He is in us and we in Him so we escape into the other dimensions, the dimensions of heaven, the dimension of the spirit.

Our Father in Heaven

Heaven is our consciousness of God, not limited by time and space – the earthly dimensions. We talk sometimes glibly, of the fourth or fifth dimensions, but these are human stretchings of the mind. Shall we say that God exists in the nth dimension, in infinity? Yet again there is the two-ness 'Heaven lies about us in our infancy', says Wordsworth 'Except you become as a little child you cannot enter the Kingdom' (Luke 9.48), and again, 'The angels of the children behold the face of my father in heaven'. The scriptures in both Old and New Testaments keep reassuring us that man is God's temple, God's dwelling place. Heaven is near at hand when we pray to the Father. Shall we remember the prayer of Solomon as he dedicated the temple: 'Will God in very deed dwell with men on the earth? Heaven and the heaven of heavens cannot contain Thee. How much less this house that I have built'.

In depth psychology we reach out into awareness of the great unconscious, stretching into infinity beyond the concepts of our knowing, of our consciousness. All through the ages men have sought to penetrate the depths and to establish open channels for the creative energy, intuitive wisdom, 'That' which makes all things possible.

Abraham was the friend of God, Moses lived in His presence, Jesus was a prince with God. Jesus as the Lord Christ seeks His way in our lives. Doors are opening today between the ultimate and the present. Many are seeking to open these doors and free the channels through meditation taught in the different schools. Also this is happening through analytic methods of psychology aiming at the conquest of fear and the liberation of creativity. Other ways are opening and will open as we ask, seek and knock *intent* on the taking, the finding, the opening up of our lives into the wider dimensions of Heaven.

Hallowed be Thy name

What name? Jehovah as He was first revealed to man? Wonderful Counsellor, the Mighty God, the Everlasting Father, the Prince of Peace – names breath-taking in their impact on our minds? Jesus has taught us that the nature and the name of God is Love. To keep this name holy in our lives, in our thoughts, and in our deeds is the task laid upon us as disciples.

'I am that I am' (Exodus 3:14) – the name that God allowed Moses to use as he taught the Israelites of His presence with them – is puzzling to our ears. Did God say 'I am that I am – take me or leave me?' Perhaps that was part of the meaning. The translation into English from the Hebrew may be faulty and something more dynamic be intended – possibly 'My name is *"Something is happening"*'. Let us watch how often His name – this expression – is on our lips at the present time. Something is happening in the world today – a summit conference, questions at the Security Council – protests in favour of human rights, indignation over the spread of work on nuclear energy. Something, too, is happening in your life and mine whenever we seek to understand rather than to blame, and to look outside ourselves i.e. to the Christ, as well as in the deeper strata of our minds for wholeness. To make His name holy we must aim at holiness in our own lives, wholeness of the body – that is, health of the mind – that is, sanity; of the spirit – that is, sanctity. It comes not of ourselves, but through the holy in-dwelling spirit of God.

A new age is dawning. Old things are passing away. In terms of modern psychology Jahweh, the God of the Jews – was largely a super-ego figure with its function of discipline. The word spoken from the mountain was 'Thou shalt ... Thou shalt not', just as modern parents early in the child's life say 'No – you ought – you ought not'. Even in the far-off days the super-ego was also conceived and understood as a guiding principle, a teacher, a presence, that which keeps mankind facing the right way, that which ultimately supports and holds, to Moses Jahweh said 'My presence shall go with thee and I will give thee rest.' (Exodus 33.14) To the psalmist the assurance came that even in the depths of His hand would guide and His right hand uphold. (Psalm 139) 'Fear not – I am with Thee' is a recurring re-assurance throughout the scripture. So we are praying that in our lives we may ever enlarge our concept of His name until it becomes *whole* and increasingly holy in our thought.

Thy Kingdom Come

A kingdom not in time or space, not 'out there', not of future time, but whenever and wherever Love conquers fear and hate in a man's heart – there the kingdom is being established. The victory of love is the coming of the kingdom – God has centred Himself in our lives. This occurs in all religions everywhere, it is the divine flame awaiting re-kindling. The Buddhists call it Enlightenment, Jung in his modern psychological teaching has taken the Self from the ancient Indian Vedic teaching – the word *Atman* – to denote the awakening of the centre deep in the psyche. No longer identified with the outer mask – the persona – with which we have been taught to face the world, but now in touch with the deep unconscious are we nourished and renewed. The kingdom is established within us.

To pray for the coming of the kingdom involves us not only in an aspiration but also with a task. We are stewards and workers. Stewards must be found faithful to their tasks of protecting their masters' property – caring for his vineyards, guarding his fields. Jesus in his teaching seemed to emphasize this aspect of our relationship with God. It *matters* whether we do much or little or even nothing at all with what is committed to us. The kingdom is like yeast *which a woman takes and hides* in three measures of meal. The yeast is a microscopic grain – to do its work each cell splits and takes on new life – something happens – the bread – the loaf – is ready to feed mankind.

The kingdom is like a tiny seed *which a man takes and hides* in the earth. Its husk – the outside covering – dies, but within the seed itself something happens – it sends roots downwards, its stem and leaf upward until it comes to itself as a great fruit-bearing tree. Yeast, grain or mustard seed – the death is only of the outer shell. Its death is symbolic, the living, life-holding kernel, the self, cannot die. Nor more can we if our life is lived through Christ in God. Because He lives we shall live also.

Thy Will be done

Thy will. How often we intercede when we are saying My will – 'Please God – *my* will, this is what I so much want'. Wanting – 'I want' are words which a child uses in his early communication. He learns inevitably that he cannot get everything he wants but still throughout life this primitive expression of our need persists. It is sad indeed when things go wrong and we say 'I don't know what I want.' This may be the result of harsh denial of the child's demands 'You can't have what you want'.

The ability to use this petition 'Thy will be done', involves a certain maturity, a willingness to relinquish our own ego-centric demands. We remember St Augustine's beautiful words 'In His will is our peace.'

Acceptance of the will differs from mere resignation to the will. We can hear ourselves and others saying 'Oh, I suppose that is God's will', we find it hard, though inevitable, and feel that we lose something by accepting it. We groan and acquiesce unwillingly. Can we see it another way? Is it not possible and indeed certain that the will of God coincides with man's total well-being? That God is co-operating with us when we catch a glimpse of what He wants of us in our daily lives? Spiritual maturity and the ability to accept joyfully come as we gain insight and wisdom. If we really long for understanding the way opens – for some it may be through literature, music or art; for others through suffering. Meditation is bringing light and understanding and its practice is available to us all. For some there are analytic psychic processes – God's ways are infinite but Jesus taught us that if we knock hard enough and persistently at the door it will be opened. (Luke 11:5-9) God's will is for mankind's highest good. Let us visualize two great streams uniting – the Love of God, and the Will of God – God's libido flowing through humanity.

On earth as it is in Heaven
Then Heaven is the place where The Will is accepted and fulfilled – here and there, everywhere, when we say 'I am willing. I am come to do they Will' – the Kingdom is established. The Lord God Omnipotent reigneth.

Give us this day our daily bread
This means our immediate need for today – for body, mind and spirit: energy-giving sustenance. There is a beautiful symbolic story in the Bible about the daily bread given to the grumbling Israelites in the desert. It was called Manna – the word is a question and means 'What is it?' They were told to go out early in the day before the sun was up and they would find golden granules like coriander seed. It was important that each man or each family gathered enough for his needs, if too much was gathered it went bad on their hands – so that each morning they must gather the day's portion. Presumably the manna had been *there all the time* but only when they *asked* for bread were they made to realize it was there. Our Lord used this story and told his disciples that he was 'the living bread' available always but we must be aware, aware of his Presence which is there all the time. (John 6:31-35)

The words *bread* and *breast* are cognate as also are the words *loaf* and *life*. When we ask for bread we acknowledge our dependence on the giver of all good things. The good mother gives her breast to the infant – wholly dependent on her for life. The Latin word for wheat is 'semen' which reminds us again of the life-giving father; in some countries the loaf has a phallic shape.

Food for the mind is also to be sought for daily.

Give us this day our daily bread, we pray
And give us likewise, Lord, our daily thought,
That our poor minds may strengthen as they ought,
And starve not on the husks of yesterday.

One of our instinctual drives is curiosity – the need to know – the epistemological instinct. So adults we well as children must ask questions and expect answers – trying always to be released from outworn opinions and ideas, keeping our minds open to what is happening in the minds and in the lives of the new generation, as well as in the minds of people of other countries, other civilizations past and present. To be truly alive and truly awake we need to seek daily for new ideas and new thoughts, just as certainly as we have need of bread.

And food for the Spirit – we hear Jesus the Christ responding to our petition – 'Take eat – this is my body' and 'I am the bread of life'. Even before the coming of Christ the bread was identified with the Word. We can hear the prophet Jeremiah saying 'They words were found and I did eat them and thy word was to me the joy and rejoicing in my heart'. (Jeremiah 15:16)

Moses too: 'We live not by bread alone but by the Word' and the Lord quoted this saying at the time of his temptation in the wilderness 'Man shall not live by bread alone but by every word that proceedeth out of the mouth of God'. 'I have esteemed the words of His mouth more than my necessary food' said poor Job in his sorrow (Job 23:12). In the apocryphal Book of Wisdom in the Old Testament there is the beautiful message 'Creation, in obedience to You its maker, became by a total transformation the agent of Your all-nourishing bounty. So that Your beloved children, Lord, might learn that the various crops are not what nourishes them, but Your word which preserves all who trust in You.'

Let us look at the manna again. Was it there all the time at dawn every day? Through God's words did they, the Israelites, become conscious of it? Just there it lies on the breast of Mother Earth, here and now, enough for each individual for one day. Gather, gather, not too much – enough. After the sunrise it disappears, so gather *now*.

Forgive us our debts as we forgive our debtors

In our Scottish presbyterian congregations we use 'debts' and 'debtors' rather than the Episcopal, and Catholic, 'Trespasses'. This is in accordance with the version given in St Matthew's gospel, followed by the enlightening parable of the debtors, of the forgiven man who could not forgive and suffered the extreme penalty.

To forgive is to give utterly as only love can give – to wipe out the debt leaving no trace. It reminds me of my early school days, each child had a slate and a small wet sponge in a little tin box. Whether you did your sums well or badly, whether they were right or wrong they were *wiped out*, obliterated, at the end of the lesson. It must have been a key-note in the *teaching* of Jesus – love and forgiveness even of enemies, but also it sheds light on the healing miracles. '*Son* thy sins are forgiven – get up and walk. *Daughter* – your sins are forgiven – your bleeding has stopped'. Was he saying 'It is guilt, your own feeling of being in the wrong which paralyzes you or which drains you so unnecessarily of your vitality?' Why don't the physicians of today heed the lesson of these miracles? Those of us who practise analytical psychotherapy witness healings in the course of our work – often very dramatically, with creative ability replacing the illness.

A patient of mine who died some years ago had suffered from almost incessant haemorrhage for twelve years (and suffered too, she said, from many physicians). She realized one day that the onset co-incided with her divorce, about which she felt very guilty. The realization was accompanied by a dream in which the priest by her side as he poured wine to the communion cups made it overflow. I still remember her saying 'Far too much – far too much – he was so foolish'. With the realization of the meaning of her own words she was healed. The rhythm of her life was re-established and the symptom never recurred – although she lived well into her post-menopausal years. Forgiveness has to be accepted, then guilt and inferiority can be discarded. Carrying our sins around with us all our lives is a fruitless, foolish way of living. Guilt and inferiority block us in all relationships, in all activity of spirit, mind and body. It is imperative, if we would live creatively, to take the reassurance, realize completely the forgiveness and get on with the joyful business of living. Preceding forgiveness is understanding 'I understand, I know myself forgiven, I am restored to health, I am well'.

When we are healed through understanding and forgiveness we find our lives made new – we are clothed with humility, with compassion, with kindness, with patience, gentleness and love. Aware, conscious of our own 'clean slate' we have no longer the compulsion to project on to others our guilt and shortcomings but rather to go out to them in love, forgiving them the hurt they have done to us, forgiving, giving utterly as only love can give. All life is a taking, a holding and giving and life makes sense to us as we discover this, can we discover ourselves as channels, as pipe lines, living growing conduits for creative energy, for love and all the good gifts for which humanity is starving, the little ones hungry, thirsty, naked, sick, imprisoned, alienated. In all these God is incarnate, all are in dire need of love, in need, let us be aware, of our service and know that in serving them we relate in ever new ways to the Giver of all life. Taking, holding, giving, make life meaningful. Without taking we are dried out wells, without giving and forgiving we are like the Dead Sea which has no outlet, in its bitterness all the little fish – all life – dies. Resentment is unforgivingness, guilt is inability to take forgiveness – in the taking and the giving we find love and peace.

The transaction is primarily between parent and child. The child is in debt to the parent for the gift of life, for the conception, the gestation, the feeding, protection, education and then the letting go. The child must at some time in his growth recognize and acknowledge his debts and so find his gratitude and right relationship. We as parents must recognize our failings without self-justification or self-righteousness. Every parent fails the child, is never the ideal parent, never gives enough, never fully understands so that resentment on the child's part and guilt on the parent's are inevitable: we cannot escape! When the child comes to maturity, when he has become truly adult, then he is able to forgive his parents and allows them to find freedom from the debtor's prison.

Whatever the number of years and whether our parents are alive or dead as long as we harbour resentment against them we are holding to our immaturity. *'If only makes no sense'* and yet we continue to think and say 'If only' – if only the parents had been wiser, kinder, more understanding, less rigid, less impatient, less stupid. There is no end to these 'if onlys' but they make no sense. We must not only tolerate our parents but accept them and forgive them and are thus more likely to become adequate parents in our turn. The young child accepts the parent at his own valuation. A young boy once said to me 'Yes. I have a good father, when he is drunk we just hide under the bed.' The adolescent criticizes and destroys the image of the perfect parent. In adulthood – if we can attain it – we find equality, we forgive their failings, recognizing their handicaps and difficulties, making resolutions about ourselves as parents. We accept them as they are, not as they might have been.

The work of psycho-therapeutic analysis is the work of understanding. *Only through understanding, grasping the meaning of individual life, do we truly find ourselves able to forgive*, no longer torn, distressed, split, but truly working towards the integration of the psyche, the wholeness of body, mind and spirit.

Lead us – not into temptation (Ezekiel 37:5-12)
The Shepherd, even today, appears very often on the landscapes of the middle Eastern countries. He leads the sheep, going ahead of his flock, so that they keep him in view and follow where he leads (Ezekiel 34.6 et seq). Throughout the scriptures we find references to the shepherd, he is an archetype ('The Lord is my shepherd'), and in the Lord's prayer we are taught to pray that the Lord will lead us, not into the wilderness to be tempted, but by the green pastures and still waters where our souls will be nourished and we may live in peace without fear.

'Put us not to the test' is one modern translation. What is the test, the temptation? Is it to lose sight of the Shepherd, to go it alone, trusting in our own virtues, losing our sense of unity with the others, substituting *I, me, mine* for *we, us, our?* Jesus was led by the Spirit into the wilderness to be tempted but we pray that he should not lead us the same way. Paul, again, has something to say about it, an assurance that we shall not be tempted beyond our strength to resist but can depend on God's faithfulness to provide a way of escape – a way out. (Cor 10:13) The three temptations which Jesus encountered are listed as: 1. To satisfy personal needs by the realization of personal power. 2. To climb too high and make foolish demands on miraculous powers. 3. To pay too high a price for power and possessions. The answers were: 1. We are utterly satisfied when we are fed by God's word. 2. We are always completely safe in God's presence. 3. All things are ours when we know ourselves his children.

Jesus in his temptation was our great example and we pray not to lose sight of him. The Jerusalem Bible has a beautiful translation (John 8-12) 'He who follows me will not be walking in the dark', and in this gospel the symbolism is used again and again to reassure us that we are cared for, that we are individuals, and that even when we are lost and wounded that His caring spirit seeks us out. The divine guidance is made alive to us in Alexander Carmichael's translation from the Gaelic of a poem *The Guardian Angel.*

Be thou a bright flame before me
Be thou a guiding star above me
Be thou a smooth path before me
And be a kindly shepherd behind me
Today, tonight and for ever.

Gospel teaching emphasizes continually *the caring spirit* of the Christ. The mission of Jesus was to the outcast, the despised, the diseased. He was not primarily interested in the complacent righteous people but in those who sinned. The Shepherd parable tells of the ninety-nine who are securely shut up in the fold (in their own righteousness) but of the Shepherd's need to search for and find and restore *the one* who gives so much trouble. *Lead us*, not into the temptation of self-righteousness, but may the caring spirit be ours wherever it may lead us.

Deliver us from evil

Set us free from the imprisoning compulsions of our lives, 'the sins that so early beset us', the behaviour patterns frozen in our deep unconscious from which we find it difficult, sometimes impossible to escape. Those of us who practise psychotherapy know how likely we are to despair over the compulsive drinkers (alcoholics), compulsive eaters, gamblers, talkers, thieves and such like. Do we know how to even begin to 'cure'? There has to be a death and a resurrection – something outside human capacity to affect.

Again listen to Paul (Corinthians 1:1-30), 'Christ Jesus is to us – freedom, and when he cries 'Who shall deliver us?' (set us free), His answer is 'Thank God it can happen through Christ'. In psychological terms we can see this as a transfer of energy from the conscious ego and its power to make decisions and choices to a deeper level, the Self, in contact with the great unconscious creative forces.

Here we get the unity of all truth, related always to the depth, to inner ultimate reality, operating creatively, coming into the awareness of man's spirit as the channel of life and love in all fulness when it is 'planted in love and built on love' invisible. By definition psychology is the wisdom of the spirit, religion the binding to the eternal values. Either way we are seeking for 'That' which ever creates anew bringing life out of death, a new structure out of the forces of destruction.

For Thine is the Kingdom, the Power and the Glory for ever Amen

These words are first attributed to King David who at the end of his life gave a great blessing to the name of the Lord and dedicated all the materials he had gathered for the building of the Temple by his son Solomon (Chron: 29:11); 'Thine O Lord is the greatness and the power and the glory and the victory and the majesty; for all that is in the heaven and in the earth is thine; Thine is the Kingdom, O Lord, and thou art exalted as King overall'.

Surrendering the omnipotence of immaturity we find instead the 'I can do all things through Christ'. Psychologically expressed we see frustration and defeat associated with our identification with the idealized image of the self, of the mask or persona, on the other hand fulfilment and victory when the true Self is established in control with creative activity in ultimate inner reality.

The Power

Christ the Power of God (1 Cor. 1:4) and the wisdom of God. God the source of all energy, of the 'intuitive wisdom', the life force, the flowing water of life – libido, through which mankind is energised and knows himself co-creative with the eternal purpose. Without this living stream, life becomes futile, sterile, limited by material things. Think again of God's will and God's love as two streams uniting to flow through humanity, through your life and mine as individuals. Our roots in the water, we bear much fruit.

The Glory

This is associated with the Presence of God. Moses was allowed to be only partly aware but thereafter his face shone, (Ex. 33). At the dedication of Solomon's temple the glory dispelled the darkness and filled the sanctuary. Throughout the ages mystics have been aware of the light and even today there is a shining on the faces of those who worship and seek God's face.

For ever

Not only in the future but *ever* includes *now* – *Now* the creative 'imperishable moment'. *Now* we lay hold on life and enter anew into His presence.

Amen

May it be so in our lives today and every day.